THE COOK'S COMPANION

THE COOK'S COMPANION

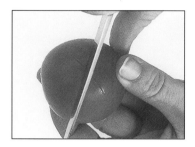 

ELIZABETH WOLF-COHEN

angus

AN OCEANA BOOK

Published by Angus Books Ltd
Swift Distribution
Units 1 – 6 Kingsnorth Industrial Estate
Hoo, Nr. Rochester
Kent ME3 9ND

ISBN 978-1-84573-295-0

QUMCCH

This book is produced by
Oceana Books
6 Blundell Street
London N7 9BH

Manufactured in Singapore by
Pica Digital Pte Ltd

Printed in China by
CT Printing Ltd

CONTENTS

HERBS, SPICES AND FLAVOURINGS

Herbs, spices and flavourings all contribute to our enjoyment of food. Although most are used in quantities too small to have much nutritional value, they add tremendous scent, flavour and colour to almost everything we cook. Vanilla, saffron, spirits and wine, give foods a distinctive character.

HERBS

Using fresh and dried herbs is a creative and healthy way to liven up the flavours of your meals. Herbs can be used in a variety of ways to give a variety of flavours. Herbs are very popular in today's cooking, and a wide variety of fresh herbs is available in supermarkets.

Leafy herbs can be divided into two groups: fragile herbs and robust herbs. Fragile herbs – parsley, tarragon, basil, chervil and mint – are tender and bruise easily. They are best coarsely chopped and eaten raw as a garnish or very lightly cooked. For longer cooking, the stalks are used to provide flavour, then removed before the dish is served.

The more robust herbs – thyme, bay leaf, rosemary, sage, savory, oregano and marjoram – have thicker, sturdier leaves, which are generally strong in flavour and aroma. Because of their strength, these herbs are usually cooked for a longer time and used in stocks and stews.

Some herbal plants, such as dill, celery, angelica, lovage, fenugreek and coriander, produce leafy herbs as well as seeds which are treated as spices. In general, the leaves are tender and fragile, and used as tender herbs. The seeds are usually crushed and cooked for a longer time.

Oregano

Parsley

Lemon thyme

Basil

Chervil

Rosemary

Sorrel

BUYING AND STORING HERBS

When buying fresh herbs, choose the healthiest, freshest-looking sprigs with a strong aroma. Avoid musty-smelling herbs with brown-yellow leaves. Buy dried herbs in small containers which can be used within a year. Store them in a cool, dry, dark place.

LARGE BUNCHES OF HERBS ON LONGER STALKS: Cut the stalk ends, stand the stalks in a jug or bottle of water, and enclose the leaves in a large plastic bag, tying it around the pitcher. Refrigerate, if possible, for several days.

FRESH HERBS WITH SHORT STALKS: Wrap the stalks in damp kitchen paper. Keep in a loosely tied plastic bag in the salad drawer of the refrigerator. They will keep for several days.

DRYING AND FREEZING HERBS

Avoid washing the leaves of fresh herbs unless necessary. Just shake them and wipe off any sand or dirt with soft kitchen paper or your fingers. Tailor-made stackable drying trays with mesh screens are available from speciality kitchen shops.

TO BUNCH-DRY HERBS: Tie the herbs together with string and hang, stalk end up, in a dry, warm spot away from direct sunlight. Allow the air to circulate and, if hanging outdoors, bring them in at night when they might hold condensation, which would encourage mould. Alternatively, individual sprigs can be laid flat on baking sheets and dried under the same conditions. Turn them occasionally; when dry, remove the leaves and pack in glass jars. Store as for dried herbs.

FREEZING UNCHOPPED HERBS:
Tie a small bundle together and dip the heads into boiling water for a few seconds. Plunge into ice water to stop cooking and help set the colour. Dry gently, remove the leaves from the stalk, and pack into small freezer bags. Add frozen herbs directly to cooked foods. The most successful results using this method are with parsley and tarragon. Basil, chives and dill do not need blanching.

MICROWAVE/OVEN DRYING:
To dry herbs in the microwave, put about 6 sprigs of herbs on a double layer of kitchen paper. Cover with another layer and microwave on full power for 2 to 3 minutes. Or, small quantities can be dried in the oven. Preheat to the lowest temperature, spread the leaves on a rack on a baking sheet lined with muslin and set in the oven. Leave door ajar and stir occasionally until the leaves are crisp and dry.

FREEZING CHOPPED HERBS: Put 1 tablespoon of chopped herbs – such as parsley, chives, dill, tarragon or coriander – into the bottom of an ice-cube tray compartment. Fill with water, making sure the herbs are covered, and freeze. To use, stir a cube of the ice-herb into stocks, soups and stews.

CHOPPING FRESH HERBS

It is the aromatic essential oils in the herb which provide flavour and aroma. Strip the leaves from their stalks for chopping; reserve the stalks for use in stocks and soups.

Pile the leaves on a cutting board and, holding a large chef's knife, rock it back and forth. Continue chopping to the required degree of fineness.

Dill

Basil

Sweet marjoram

MAKING A BOUQUET GARNI

A *bouquet garni* is one of the most important aromatics in the kitchen. It is used to flavour stocks and many long-cooked stews and braises. A classic bouquet is made with fresh parsley stalks, thyme sprigs and bay leaves, although a stalk of celery or leek is sometimes added. Little bouquet garnis of dried herbs can be bought, but the flavour of a home-made one is superior. Tie the herbs with string, which can be used to remove the bouquet before serving the dish.

THE ONION FAMILY

Although technically vegetables, the onion family is used to provide some of our most common flavourings: onion itself, garlic, shallots, leeks and chives, the only true herb of the family. Garlic has a somewhat controversial flavour – some people love it; others avoid it at all costs. It is known for its pungency, aroma and blood-thinning properties, and is used extensively in Mediterranean and Asian cooking. Although it can be roasted as a vegetable, it is most often used in small quantities to enhance other flavours. There are three kinds of garlic: white – the most commonly seen variety – purple and red-skinned. They range in flavour from mild to strong, the freshest being the mildest. Elephant garlic, a giant mild variety, is becoming widely available and is ideal for roasting whole as a vegetable.

COOKING WITH GARLIC

Garlic can be used raw in salad dressings, marinades and dips, or it can be cooked in many dishes. It is frequently added to lightly sautéed onions as a base for many other food preparations. After long cooking, the flavour softens and sweetens. Do not allow it to brown when cooking, as it develops a bitter taste.

FRYING GARLIC: If frying garlic with onions, first cook the onions slowly over a medium heat in 1–2 tablespoons of butter or oil. Stir in the chopped garlic and cook only 1 minute or until just softened and fragrant. Proceed as recipe directs. *Do not allow to brown.*

AS A FLAVOURING: To use as a flavouring only, heat 2 tablespoons (or more) of oil in a skillet over medium-low heat. Add a few garlic cloves and cook slowly, stirring frequently, until soft and lightly coloured. Remove the garlic and add the remaining ingredients as directed.

PEELING AND CHOPPING GARLIC

If the garlic is old and has begun to germinate, remove the green centre
heart since it has a bitter taste.

SEPARATING CLOVES:
To separate the individual cloves, crush the
bulb with the palm of your hand, or pull off
individual cloves with your fingers.

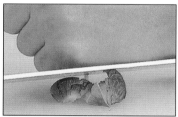

CRUSHING GARLIC:
To crush a clove of garlic with a knife, set
the blade of a large chef's knife on top of the
clove and pound with the side of your fist.
Remove the skin.

CHOPPING GARLIC:
To hand-chop garlic, peel off the papery skin,
cut off the top and root end, and chop
coarsely or finely with the blade of the knife,
as for leafy herbs. Or, chop as for shallots.

BUSY COOKS

Put peeled cloves in a garlic crusher. Squeeze the handles together, pushing
the pulp out of the crusher. Use only where a very strong flavour is required.

SHALLOTS

The shallot, a purple-green vegetable, is a variety of onion. Most frequently used in French cooking, it should never be allowed to brown or it will become bitter, like burnt garlic. Finely chopped, it can be used raw in salad dressings or marinades, or as a base for fine-flavoured sauces.

PREPARING SHALLOTS:
1 Using a small, sharp knife, peel the shallot by cutting off the stem and root ends and pull off the brown skin. Sometimes there are 2 sections; separate, if necessary, and set each section, flat-side down, on a cutting board.

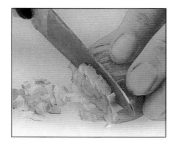

2 Slice lengthways through the shallot just to the root end, but not cutting through it. Pressing down on the curved side with your fingers, slice horizontally in towards the root end, leaving the slices attached.

3 Cut crossways, allowing the shallot to fall into finely diced pieces.

CHIVES

Chives have a lovely, mild, onion flavour and look pretty as a garnish, whether snipped, chopped or used whole. Chives are best used fresh. They can be frozen in small plastic bags and used right out of the freezer also.

PREPARING CHIVES:
1 Using kitchen scissors, hold a small bunch of chives over a bowl and snip into small pieces.

2 Or, with a knife, chop or slice crossways into tiny pieces.

BUYING AND USING SPICES

Nowadays, most spices are widely available in supermarkets and are sold whole or ground. Buy in small quantities because they lose their potency. Whole spices will keep longer than ground spices. Store in tightly sealed jars in a cool, dry, dark place. Store red spices – such as paprika, cayenne and dried red pepper flakes – in the refrigerator, where they will keep their strength and colour longer.

The cuisines of the hot countries such as India, North Africa, Africa, Latin America and Indonesia, use spices most lavishly, perhaps because many spices originate in these countries. Northern and Central Europe use "fragrant" and some "hot" spices, such as cinnamon, nutmeg, and cloves, seeds like dill and juniper, and paprika. French and Italian cooking tends to use fresh herbs more than spices, and the Chinese and Japanese use garlic, soy, and ginger more than any other spices.

However, there are several traditional spice mixtures that can be bought or made at home. Curry powder, *garam masala* (a traditional Indian spice mixture), American chilli powder, Chinese five-spice powder, French *quatre-épices* (four spices), and the North African *ras-el-hanout* are all better prepared at home with freshly ground spices. Hot spices, such as pepper, mustard, chilli peppers and ginger add an intense heat and individual flavour to many dishes. These spices need careful preparation and temperate use because they can be overpowering.

MAKING A SPICE BAG

To make a spice bag for pickling or other long-cooked dishes, wrap the whole spices in a square of muslin. Pull the edges together and tie with string, leaving one end long enough to tie to the handle of a cooking utensil. This allows the bag to be found and easily removed at the end of the cooking time.

TOASTING SPICES

To toast whole spices before grinding, put them in a heavy-based frying pan and toast over low heat, shaking and stirring gently until they are fragrant. Be careful not to burn them as they scorch easily. Transfer to a plate to cool before grinding.

GRINDING SPICES

Use a pestle and mortar to grind spices, or a small electric coffee grinder; but reserve it for spice-grinding only. To coarsely grind or crack spices, put them in a heavy-duty freezer bag and twist to close. Crush the spices with a heavy pan or rolling pin.

PEPPER

Peppercorns can be black, white or green. Black pepper is the dried unripe berry. White pepper is the dried ripened berry, with the outer casing removed. It is less intense than black pepper and often used in cream sauces. Green peppercorns are unripe pepper berries which have a slightly acid taste. They are available preserved in brine or freeze-dried. Green peppercorns preserved in brine should be rinsed and used in cream sauces for steaks or with other rich meats like duck or venison. If using freeze-dried berries, crush lightly.

Pink peppercorns come from a South American plant related to poison ivy. They have a slightly sharp, acidic flavour, but are primarily used for a decorative effect. Szechuan pepper is a dried berry. Its unique aroma is prized in Chinese cooking. It should be lightly toasted before crushing.

MUSTARD

Dijon

Mustard can be made from black, white or brown seeds. Black mustard seeds have the finest flavour, but are difficult to harvest and have largely been replaced by brown seeds, which are more suitable for mechanical production. Yellow seeds, used in most American mustards, are the mildest. Whole seeds appear in pickles, relishes and chutneys, and in Indian cooking. Ground mustard is mixed with liquid to make prepared mustard. All are used as condiments and in cooking.

American mustard

Store all mustard in a cool, dry place for up to a year. Refrigerate any opened prepared mustard.

One of the most famous prepared mustards is *Dijon*. It must conform to a certain standard, following a strict recipe of ground black mustard seeds, salt, spices and wine or wine vinegar.

German mustard

American mustard is made from yellow mustard seed, salt, vinegar and spices. The addition of turmeric gives it the bright yellow colour associated with American hot dogs.

Most *German mustards* are dark, smooth and slightly sweet, the result of added caramel.

Coarse-grain mustard

English mustard is made from a combination of ground dark and light seeds, and is smooth, bright yellow and very hot. In its powdered form, dry mustard is added to mayonnaise, cheese sauces and other sauces and dressings.

Chinese mustard is also very hot and sharp. It is sold as a powder for mixing with water or other liquid and as a condiment or dipping sauce.

Coarse-grain mustards are produced in many countries. The rough texture comes from coarsely ground seeds blended into the mixture.

COOKING WITH MUSTARD

English mustard

MAKING PREPARED MUSTARDS:
To make prepared mustard from dry mustard powder, blend an equal amount of water, wine, milk or beer into the measured amount of mustard powder. Allow to stand 10–15 minutes for full flavour to develop.

USING PREPARED MUSTARDS:
Add prepared mustards to cream sauces or gravy by whisking in just before the end of cooking time. Prolonged cooking inhibits the flavour and intensity of the mustard.

CHILLIES

There are dozens of varieties of fresh peppers, both hot and sweet. Although sweet peppers are usually treated as vegetables, chillies are more often used in small quantities as a spicy flavouring. They range in flavour, colour and degree of hotness. Most of the heat is contained in the seeds and veins. The powerful oils in chilli can burn eyes and other sensitive areas, so use rubber gloves when preparing chillies and wash all utensils and surfaces well after any contact.

Hot red pepper flakes and *crushed red pepper* are made from dried, crushed chillies. They are slightly milder than fresh chilli.

Cayenne pepper is a very fine chilli powder with a very fiery heat. It is used in very small quantities.

Paprika is ground from European varieties of sweet peppers. Hungary produces the most flavourful paprikas, ranging from mild and sweet to hot and spicy, used in the famous Hungarian goulash. Also popular in Spain, the seeds and veins are removed before grinding. *Hot red pepper sauce* (such as Tabasco sauce) is the liquid of salted ground chillies, matured for up to 3 years before bottling. It is used in soups, stews and Creole and Mexican dishes.

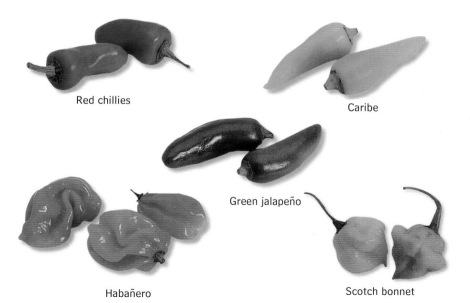

Red chillies

Caribe

Green jalapeño

Habañero

Scotch bonnet

PREPARING CHILLIES

For a relatively mild, yet spicy flavour, core the chillies and remove the seeds before chopping. Wash hands and all equipment thoroughly after use, and wear rubber or plastic gloves.

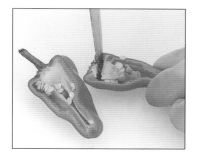

Red jalapeño

1 Using a small, sharp knife, cut the chilli in half lengthways. Scrape out the seeds and remove the white veins from the sides.

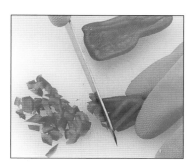

Bird's eye

2 Cut into strips lengthways, then slice or chop into small pieces.

ALTERNATIVES

Commercial dried chilli can be substituted for fresh. If you like, cut off the stalk, shake out the seeds and put the pepper in a small bowl. Cover with warm water, soak for about 30 minutes, then drain.

GINGER

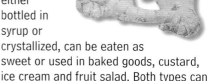

Fresh ginger

This underground stalk, or rhizome, is available fresh, dried, ground, pickled, candied whole or crystallized. Its hot yet sweet flavour is essential in Chinese and Indian cooking. Fresh ginger should look plump with a creamy beige colour and thin skin. After peeling, it can be grated, chopped or sliced, and used in sweet and savoury dishes. The root can also be dried and grated for use in baking. To keep for up to 3 weeks, wrap in kitchen paper in a plastic bag and store in the refrigerator.

Pickled ginger in vinegar is a pink, tangy condiment used to accompany Japanese sushi. Preserved ginger, either bottled in syrup or crystallized, can be eaten as sweet or used in baked goods, custard, ice cream and fruit salad. Both types can be found in most supermarkets.

Liquorice ginger is another variety of preserved ginger. Seasoned with salt and sugar, rhizome liquorice is used in Chinese fish dishes. It is found in Chinese supermarkets.

Ground ginger

Pickled ginger

Crystallized ginger

Stem ginger

PREPARING FRESH GINGER

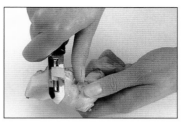

PEELING AND CHOPPING:
Using a swivel-bladed vegetable peeler, peel the outside skin exposing the smooth root. Cut lengthways into thin slices; then cut crossways and continue chopping into small pieces.

JULIENNING:
Cut lengthways into thin slices, then cut lengthways again into thin julienne strips.

GRATING:
Rub the peeled ginger against the fine side of a cheese grater. Use the juice as well as the flesh.

HORSERADISH

Horseradish is a very powerful root related to the cabbage family. Native to Eastern Europe, it is used raw, either grated as a condiment or in other condiments, such as seafood sauces.

Prepared horseradish is preserved in vinegar and is the traditional accompaniment to *gefilte fish*, a Jewish festival dish. It is sometimes mixed with beets and called *chrein*. Mixed with whipped or sour cream, it is a classic accompaniment to roast beef, boiled meats and smoked fish. Heat destroys its flavour, so it is served in cold sauces.

GRATING FRESH HORSERADISH

Horseradish is so strong it is difficult to grate by hand, since the fumes can cause painful tearfulness. Use the food processor fitted with the grater disk to grate the peeled root. *Do not open the cover.* Allow the grated horseradish to stand for 3–5 minutes, then remove the top, holding it away from you; the fumes can be very powerful.

SALT AND SALTY FLAVOURINGS

Salt is an indispensable seasoning for foods, but it must be used carefully. Serious oversalting cannot be remedied, although a little cream, milk, potato or rice may help to balance the flavour somewhat. Most foods or sauces should be salted at the beginning of cooking, so flavours blend into other ingredients. Stocks and sauces that are reduced to concentrate flavour should not be salted until the end of cooking, if at all. Salty ingredients such as bacon and cheese may negate the need for salt. Use in bread and pastry-making both to bring out flavour and to inhibit the yeast. Salt also attracts moisture, so it is used to degorge eggplants and cucumbers. For the same reason, meat should be seasoned just before cooking, since the salt draws out the juices. Salty flavourings include soy sauce and meat and yeast extracts.

SALT GLOSSARY

Table salt Soft, fine, sea, or mined salt, the most commonly used condiment, which dissolves instantly. Most table salt has iodine added.

Coarse sea salt Large, irregular crystals, free from additives and iodine, with a "less salty" taste – for sprinkling large areas or salting large quantities of water.

Sea or bay salt Refined from evaporated salts of shallow salt water pans, considered superior to table salt. The greyish French *gros sel* is considered the best.

Rock salt Roughly crushed chunks of mined salt, used in ice cream makers and for displaying seafood.

Flavoured salts Salts flavoured with celery, onion, garlic or sesame; used to season certain foods.

Sour salt Not a true salt, but crystallized citric acid of citric salt, lemon or lime, used in Middle Eastern cooking.

Light salts/salt substitutes For use in salt-restricted diets, these contain potassium and/or sodium chloride.

Sea salt

Bay salt

Rock salt

Onion salt

Garlic salt

SOY SAUCE

Celery salt

Soy sauce is made from naturally fermented soy beans and wheat which have been salted, then aged to mature and develop flavour.

Light soy sauce is paler in colour, but saltier than dark soy sauce. It is best for cooking.

Dark soy sauce is aged longer, giving it a richer hue and thicker consistency. It is used in more robust dishes and as a dipping sauce.

Light soy

Japanese soy sauce, called *shoyu*, is generally considered superior, as it is always naturally fermented.

FISH SAUCES

Dark soy

Many Asian cuisines use a fermented fish sauce to give a salty flavour to food. The Thai *nam pla* and Vietnamese *nuoc nam* are the most widely available. They are used in savoury dishes and as dips for fried foods.

Oyster sauce is a Chinese fish sauce made from oysters and wheat, corn or rice.

Anchovy paste, made from mashed, salted anchovies, gives a salty but surprisingly "non-fishy" flavour to many meat, vegetable and fish dishes.

nam pla

OLIVES AND CAPERS, ESSENCES AND EXTRACTS

In addition to being excellent finger food, olives contribute a pungent flavour to many salads, pizzas, pasta sauces and meat and duck dishes. They are also the source of nature's most delicious oils. Olives can be black (ripe) or green (unripe), large or small, brine-cured, dry-salt-cured, or a combination. Capers have a sharp, salty flavour which enhances many dishes.

ESSENCES AND EXTRACTS

Essences and extracts used to flavour food come from aromatic plant oils. Nowadays, many are produced synthetically. These flavourings are highly volatile and dissipate quickly in air or when exposed to heat, so they should be added to cold or cooling foods. When used in cakes and biscuits, cream them into the butter or fat, which slows their vapourization. In general, 1 teaspoon essence is used to flavour 450 ml (³/₄ pint) liquid or 450 g (1 lb) dry ingredients, but this depends on the recipe and personal taste. Vanilla and almond are probably the most commonly used extracts, although lemon, mint, spearmint, cinnamon and clove are also popular. Flower-based extracts, such as rosewater and orangeflower water, are used in Middle Eastern, Indian and Mediterranean cooking. They have a powerful perfume. Flower waters and all essences and extracts should be stored in a cool, dark place, preferably in dark bottles.

OLIVES

Olives are one of the world's oldest fruits and there are hundreds of different varieties. The only difference between green olives and black olives is ripeness. Unripe olives are green and fully ripe olives are black. Green olives are usually pitted, and often stuffed with various fillings, including pimientos, almonds, anchovies, jalapeños, onions or capers.

CAPERS

USING CAPERS:
Capers are the pickled buds of the Mediterranean caperberry plant. They are always cured in salt or vinegar. Care is needed since heat brings out the saltiness. Rinse and drain capers before adding to the dishes at the end of their cooking time.

VANILLA

Vanilla is probably the most frequently used flavour in baking. The so-called vanilla bean is the pod of a tropical orchid. Picked unripe and sun-cured for up to a year to release its rich flavour, these long, black beans are essential for flavouring ice creams, custards, sauces and syrups. If used to infuse a syrup or custard, the pod can be rinsed, drained, dried and used again.

PREPARING VANILLA:
1 Using a small, sharp knife, split the vanilla bean lengthways. Use to infuse hot liquid such as milk or a sugar syrup for 20–30 minutes.

2 For a stronger flavour, split the bean and, using the tip of the knife, scrape out the seeds. Add to liquids for ice creams, puddings, and custards.

VANILLA SUGAR:
Push a split vanilla bean into a 450g (1lb) jar of sugar and leave, covered, for 2–3 days or longer. Use to flavour any recipe where a hint of vanilla is called for.

FLAVOURING WITH WINES AND SPIRITS

WINE

Wine can add great substance to many dishes, but unless it is reduced during cooking, it can impart a harsh, raw or acidic taste. Some of the alcohol must be cooked out during long cooking, as in stews and braised dishes, or the wine can be reduced on the hob to concentrate its flavour in sauces. The characteristics of the wine will be intensified in cooking, so follow the rule that if a wine is good enough to drink, you can cook with it. Use robust red wines for red meat and game, roasts, rich brown sauce and gravy, and lighter red or white wines for veal, chicken and fish. Avoid using wine with salty or smoked foods and those with strong citrus flavours.

SPIRITS, BRANDIES AND LIQUEURS

Spirits and brandies are used at the start of cooking to add flavour and body to a dish, or just before serving to accentuate a robust flavour. They are often used in meat pâtés and terrines, as well as fruitcakes, and they act as a preservative. Fortified wines such as sherry, port, Madeira and Marsala are often added to sauces at the end of cooking or to deglaze pans. Liqueurs and cordials are used in desserts. If used with a stronger spirit, they can be flambéed.

DEGLAZING A PAN

To deglaze a pan, remove any cooked meats, then pour off excess fat. Add the wine or spirits, scraping up all the bits on the bottom of the pan.

REDUCING WINE

1 To reduce and concentrate wine, add it as all or part of the cooking liquid to meat or game dishes. The long, slow cooking will evaporate the alcohol naturally, leaving a concentrated wine flavour.

2 To reduce wine for use in sauces or for deglazing, pour into a saucepan and allow it to reduce by half at a simmer over medium-high heat.

FLAMBÉ

1 Heat the spirit, brandy, or liqueur in a small saucepan or ladle over a medium-high heat until bubbles form around the edge; do not boil.

2 Light the liquid with a long candle or extra-long match.

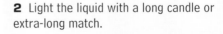

3 Pour over the heated food (crêpes, Christmas pudding, steaks and so on) and spoon over, basting the food, until the flames die out, which will happen as soon as the alcohol is evaporated.

VINEGAR

Vinegar, from the French *vin aigre* or "sour wine," can be a versatile flavouring. Vinegar is created when a naturally fermented alcohol such as wine, sherry or cider is converted to acetic acid by adding a bacteria. Nowadays this is done under controlled conditions to produce vinegar.

Commonly used in salad dressings, pickles, preserves and chutneys, it is also important for adding zest to sauces and as a tenderizer in marinades. Flavoured vinegars are ideal for deglazing cooking juices of rich meats, such as liver and duck. Store vinegars in a cool, dark place, since their flavour dissipates with age. Vinegars vary in strength (degrees of acidity) and flavour. Roughly speaking, the degree of acetic acid in vinegar will be the same as the degree of wine which produces it. Most wine vinegars will be 5 to 6 percent acetic acid.

MAKING HERB VINEGARS

Use a good quality white or red wine vinegar, or cider vinegar. Lightly bruise the herbs first to allow them to give off their flavours.

1 Put about 60 g (2oz) fresh, lightly bruised herbs in a sterilized heatproof bottle or jar. Heat about 450ml/16 fl oz vinegar until bubbles begin to form around the edge and pour over the herbs.

2 Seal and store in a cool, dark place for at least 2 weeks. Turn the bottle occasionally.

3 If you like, add a sprig of the same fresh herb to a pretty bottle, for an attractive presentation and identification. Strain the flavoured vinegar through a paper coffee filter or a muslin-lined strainer in the bottle. Seal the bottle tightly, label, and store in a cool, dark place for up to a year.

VINEGAR GLOSSARY

Wine vinegar Red or white, most wine vinegars have about 6 percent acetic acid and a pleasant wine aroma and pungency without being too harsh. Use in salad dressings, marinades, pickles and sauces.

Sherry vinegar A highly prized vinegar made from Spanish sherry, with a fragrant, nutty flavour. Use in salad dressings, sprinkled over vegetables, or to deglaze sautéed calf or chicken livers.

Raspberry and other fruit vinegars Made by marinating raspberries or other fruit in wine vinegar, before straining. Fruit-flavour vinegars add character to salad dressings, chicken, duck and liver dishes, and even to fruit salads.

Cider vinegar A milder vinegar made from apple ciders, it is especially good in dressing for coleslaws and other vegetables, as well as in pickles and milder chutneys.

White (distilled) vinegar A harsh vinegar made from grain alcohol. Widely used for pickles and chutney.

Rice vinegar Made from rice, this vinegar has a pale to clear colour with a mild, sweet flavour. Used in Chinese and Japanese cooking, it is excellent in salad dressings, dipping sauces, noodle dishes and pickles.

Balsamic vinegar Extremely popular, this highly prized vinegar is made from white grape juice aged for years in wooden casks. It becomes dark brown and almost syrupy, with a sweet-and-sour flavour. It is excellent for sprinkling on broiled vegetables or salads and even strawberries. The finest aged vinegars from Modena, Italy, can be ten years old and as expensive as fine wines.

Raspberry vinegar   Sherry vinegar   Wine vinegar

Balsamic vinegar   Cider vinegar   Rice vinegar

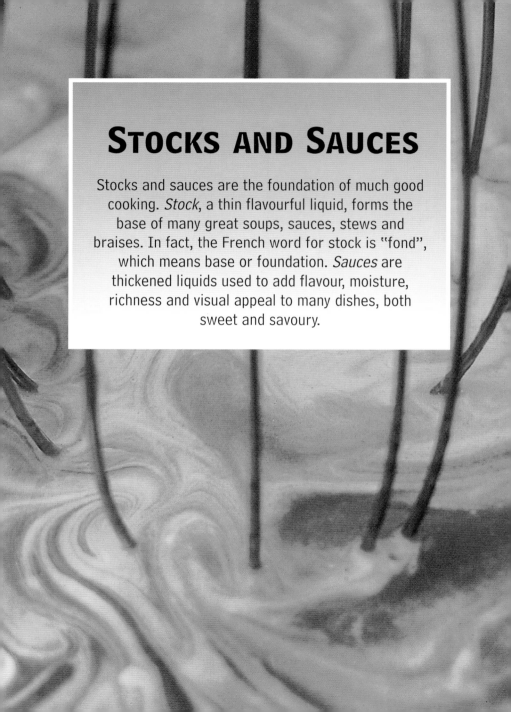

STOCKS AND SAUCES

Stocks and sauces are the foundation of much good cooking. *Stock*, a thin flavourful liquid, forms the base of many great soups, sauces, stews and braises. In fact, the French word for stock is "fond", which means base or foundation. *Sauces* are thickened liquids used to add flavour, moisture, richness and visual appeal to many dishes, both sweet and savoury.

TYPES OF STOCK

There are four basic kinds of stock which, although they use similar combinations of the same ingredients, have different characteristics. *White stocks* are not really white but pale. They are generally made by simmering beef, veal or chicken bones in water with vegetables and seasonings. The stock is pale in colour with a mild but rich flavour. Peel the onions if you want a very pale stock.

Brown stock is made from beef, veal, chicken or game bones in water with vegetables and seasonings. These are browned and caramelized first before being simmered. The stock has a rich, dark colour and a full flavour.

Fish stock or fumet is slightly different in that it cooks for a relatively short period of time, about 25 minutes. The bones are not browned, and wine or lemon juice is usually added, resulting in a pale but strongly flavoured stock. *Shellfish stock* can be made like fish stock, or the carcasses of the crustaceans can be browned in oil before simmering; it depends on its intended use.

Court bouillon is a pale, vegetable-based stock, which contains wine. It is usually cooled before being used to poach fish or delicate meats like sweetbreads.

STOCK INGREDIENTS

The basic stock ingredients are bones, vegetables, aromatics, seasoning and water. Bones are the most important ingredient, providing flavour, richness and colour. It is becoming more and more difficult to find beef and veal bones, so buy them when they are available and keep them in the freezer until you have enough to make a large pot of beef stock. Beef- and veal-based stocks need 6–8 hours; chicken stock will take 5–6 hours.

The best bones for fish stock are from lean white fish like sole, plaice, turbot and whiting. Do not use oily or strong-flavoured fish like salmon, swordfish, tuna or mackerel. Avoid large pieces of skin as they can impart bitterness to the stock. Make stocks from turkey, lamb and ham bones only for recipes using these ingredients.

Onions, carrots, celery, leeks, mushrooms and tomatoes are the most commonly used stock vegetables. It is unnecessary to peel them; in fact, onion skins are often added to give brown stock extra colour. Vegetables like cabbage, broccoli, peppers, turnips and others with easily detectable flavours are not suitable.

WHITE STOCK: WHITE VEAL STOCK

Use veal, beef or chicken bones or a combination of all of them, cut into pieces. Always try to include at least one veal bone. Bones for white stock can be blanched, if you like. Cover with cold water, and bring to the boil, skimming off the foam as it rises to the surface. Drain and rinse, then start the stock.

INGREDIENTS

1.8–2.5 kg (4–5 lb) veal bones,
    cracked or cut in pieces
2 large onions, trimmed but unpeeled
    and quartered
3 carrots, cut in 7.5–10cm (3–4in)
    pieces
1–2 celery stalks, cut into pieces
2 leeks, washed and cut in 7.5–10cm
    (3–4in) pieces
1–2 cloves garlic, crushed
large bouquet garni (see page 10)
1 tablespoon black peppercorns

1 Blanch the veal bones, if desired, following the directions above. Put the bones and all remaining ingredients into a large stockpot. Add enough cold water to cover all ingredients by at least 2.5cm (1in).

2 Set the stockpot over a medium-high heat and bring to the boil. As liquid comes to the boil, skim off any foam which rises to the surface. Reduce heat to very low and simmer for about 6 hours, skimming occasionally. The liquid should barely simmer.

3 Ladle the stock through a muslin-lined sieve or colander into a large bowl. Cool, as quickly as possible, then refrigerate.

4 When stock is chilled, use a spoon to scrape and lift the solidified fat off the surface. Store stock in the refrigerator for up to 5 days or freeze up to a year. Bring to the boil before using in other recipes.

5 For easier storage, reduce the stock to half its volume by boiling over high heat. Cool, then chill. Freeze in small quantities in plastic freezer bags or ice-cube trays. To use, dilute with as much water as required.

STOCK VARIATIONS

Chicken stock Substitute about 1.3 kg (3lb) of chicken necks and backs for half the veal bones and proceed as for White Veal Stock. Simmer for 4–5 hours.
Beef stock Substitute 1.3 kg (3lb) of beef bones for half the veal bones, or replace all veal bones with beef bones.
Brown chicken stock Substitute 1.3 kg (3lb) of chicken necks and backs for half the veal bones and proceed as for White Veal Stock, first browning the meat and bones, which gives this stock its richer colour.
Vegetable stock A good vegetable stock can be made using a wide variety of vegetables in even proportions. Brown them, if you like, before adding water; this gives the stock a richer flavour. Add a little tomato paste for colour.

BROWN STOCK:
BROWN VEAL/BEEF STOCK

Use the same ingredients as for White Stock, adding 2 halved tomatoes, and proceed as follows: Cut a third onion in half and singe; see Step 1.

Preheat oven to 230°C (450°F/Gas 8). Put the bones in a large roasting tin and roast until well browned, about 45 minutes, turning occasionally.

1 Add the cut-up vegetables, except for the tomatoes, and roast 20 minutes longer, until browned. For extra colour, hold half an onion over an electric or gas burner until completely toasted.

2 Transfer browned bones and vegetables to a large stockpot. Add the onion and remaining tomatoes, the bouquet garni and the seasonings. Set the roasting pan over direct heat. Skim off any fat, add 473 ml (16 fl oz) water and bring to the boil, stirring to deglaze the pan.

3 Pour into the stockpot and add enough cold water to cover the bones. Bring to the boil, skimming off any foam which rises to the surface. Proceed as for White Veal Stock.

FISH STOCK

Be sure to wash the fish bones well before using for stock. Do not blanch them, as blanching removes too much flavour. Sauté fish bones lightly beforehand in a little oil or butter to bring out even more flavour. If a completely fat-free stock is required, put all the ingredients, except the oil or butter, into the stockpot. Cover with enough cold water and begin at Step 3 of Brown Stock.

1 Heat about 1 tablespoon oil or butter in a large stockpot over medium heat. Add a finely chopped onion (or 3–4 finely chopped shallots). Cook 3–4 minutes until softened but not browned. Add a chopped leek, carrot, celery stalk and 115g (4oz) chopped mushrooms. Cook 3–4 more minutes.

2 Add about 725g (1$^1/_2$ lb) cut-up fish bones and stir well. Cook 2–3 minutes, then add 225ml (8 fl oz) dry white wine or the juice of half a lemon and enough cold water to cover. Drop in a bouquet garni and 1 teaspoon of lightly crushed peppercorns.

3 Bring to the boil and skim off any foam which rises to the surface. Reduce the heat to low and simmer for 20–25 minutes. Strain as for Veal Stock. Cool, then refrigerate.

SAUCES

Sauces are seasoned, thickened liquids which should have good texture, firm body and full flavour, but should not overpower the food they accompany. There are many kinds, but most fall into two categories; *thickened* and *emulsified* sauces. Others vary from a simple melted or clarified butter to sophisticated purées and reductions.

THICKENED SAUCES

A *roux*, a cooked paste of equal amounts of fat and flour, is the most commonly used thickener for white sauces (*béchamel* and *velouté*) and brown sauces. Cook a roux over medium heat before adding liquid, to eliminate any raw, floury taste and to help prevent lumps forming. A white roux should be cooked for about 1 minute, a blond or straw-coloured roux, for 2–3 minutes, and a brown roux – often used in Creole or Cajun cooking – for 10 minutes or longer to brown sufficiently.

EMULSIFIED SAUCES

Emulsified sauces include ingredients – most often, egg or egg yolks and a fat such as butter or oil – which normally do not form a stable suspension or mixture. By vigorous beating or shaking, the ingredients can be *emulsified* to form a smooth sauce in stable suspension. The most important emulsified sauces are *Hollandaise*, a warm sauce, and *mayonnaise*, a cold emulsified sauce. *Béarnaise* is made the same way as Hollandaise, but is flavoured with a reduction of vinegar, shallots and tarragon, which gives it a characteristic sweet/tangy flavour. White butter sauces, popular with chefs since nouvelle cuisine, are made without egg yolks and so have more of a tendency to separate. The quality of all these sauces depends on using the best eggs and butter or oil. Emulsified sauces are famous for being difficult because they separate or curdle so easily.

DIFFERENT METHODS FOR THICKENING SAUCES

Some sauces are best thickened at the last minute. Last minute thickeners include cornflour, arrowroot and kneaded butter (*beurre manié*). An egg and cream mixture can also be used to thicken and enrich a sauce at the last minute.

TO MAKE A ROUX:
Melt butter or oil in a heavy-based saucepan over medium heat. Add the flour all at once and stir to make a smooth paste which bubbles and foams. Cook the roux or paste for 1–10 minutes, depending on the colour desired, stirring constantly.

TO THICKEN A SAUCE WITH CORNFLOUR, ARROWROOT OR POTATO STARCH:
Dissolve 2–3 teaspoons starch with 2–3 teaspoons cold water or stock, stirring to form a paste. Gradually stir into the boiling liquid. It will thicken almost immediately. Chinese stir-fries and fruit sauces are often thickened this way.

TO THICKEN WITH KNEADED BUTTER:
Use a fork to cream together equal quantities of softened butter and flour. Whisk small pieces of kneaded butter into the boiling sauce, continuing to add small pieces of the kneaded butter until the sauce is thickened to the desired consistency. 25g (1oz) kneaded butter will thicken about 225ml (8 fl oz) liquid. It will also enrich the taste and texture.

TO THICKEN WITH AN EGG AND CREAM MIXTURE:
Beat 1 egg yolk into 2 tablespoons double cream. Bring 450ml (16 fl oz) thin sauce or liquid to the boil. Stir a little of the hot sauce into the egg mixture. Then remove the sauce from the heat and whisk the egg mixture into the sauce. Return the pan to the heat, whisking constantly until the sauce thickens. Do not boil unless the sauce contains flour to stabilize it. Serve immediately, as this sauce is difficult to reheat.

WHITE SAUCE: BÉCHAMEL SAUCE

Because of their neutral base, white sauces are extremely versatile. They are used to bind soufflés, croquettes, soups, egg dishes and gratins, and to coat many foods. The texture should be smooth and rich, and have the consistency of double cream. The taste should be milky, with no hint of raw flour. A plain white sauce or Béchamel is made with butter, flour and milk. Sometimes a clove-studded onion will be added to infuse the milk before making the sauce, or a small amount of finely chopped onion, which is sautéed in the butter or oil before adding the flour.

INGREDIENTS

225ml (8 fl oz) milk
1 onion, cut into halves and studded
  with 4 whole cloves (optional)
1 bay leaf (optional)
40g (1¹/₂ oz) butter
1¹/₂ tablespoons plain flour
pinch of grated nutmeg
salt and white pepper

For Thin White Sauce or Béchamel (to thicken soups or sauces) Use 15g (¹/₂ oz) butter and 15g (¹/₂ oz) flour to thicken 225ml (8 fl oz) milk.
For Thick White Sauce or Béchamel (to bind soufflés, etc.) Use 25g (1oz) butter and 25g (1oz) flour to thicken 225ml (8 fl oz) milk.

1 (For plain white sauce, omit this step completely.) Put the milk in a saucepan with the clove-studded onion halves, peppercorns and bay leaf. Bring to the boil over medium heat, stirring occasionally to prevent sticking. Remove from the heat. Leave to infuse, covered, for 15 minutes.

2 Melt the butter in a medium saucepan over medium-high heat. Add the flour and whisk constantly until blended and foaming, about 1 minute.

3 Gradually strain the milk into the roux and bring back to the boil. Boil for 1 minute, whisking constantly, until the sauce thickens. Season with the nutmeg, salt and pepper; simmer for 5–10 minutes. The sauce can be used immediately.

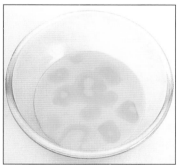

4 If not using immediately, strain or pour into a bowl. Dot the surface with flakes of butter; as the butter melts over the surface it prevents a skin from forming. Alternatively, press cling film directly against the surface to prevent a skin from forming.

CLARIFYING BUTTER

Clarified butter is a way of separating the milky solids (whey) from the pure butterfat. Once clarified, it can be served as a simple sauce, used for frying, or to help stabilize sauces like Hollandaise and Béarnaise.

1 Put the butter in a small pan and melt over low heat; do not allow the butter to boil.

2 Remove from the heat and tilt the pan slightly. Using a flat spoon, skim off any foam from the surface. Pour into a small bowl, leaving the milky solids behind. Cool, if recipe directs.

VELOUTÉ

A velouté is often made from the liquid used in cooking the main ingredient, such as that used in poaching fish and chicken, or for veal, as in a blanquette. Additional liquid is added to the roux at the beginning to make a very thin sauce. Simmering for 15 minutes to 1 hour thickens the sauce and intensifies the flavour. The long, slow cooking gives it a velvety consistency – hence the name velouté, or "velvety". Stir the sauce frequently to prevent scorching and skim from time to time.

INGREDIENTS

350ml (12 fl oz) white veal, chicken, or fish stock
40g (1$^{1}/_{2}$oz) butter
1$^{1}/_{2}$ tablespoons all-purpose flour
2–3 tablespoons double cream or crème fraîche (optional)
$^{1}/_{2}$ teaspoon lemon juice
salt and white pepper

1

2

1 Melt the butter in a heavy-based saucepan over medium heat. Pour in the flour and whisk until blended and foaming. Cook until the roux is a golden straw colour, 2–3 minutes, stirring constantly. Remove the pan from the heat and cool slightly.

2 Whisk in the stock and return the pan to the heat. Bring to the boil, whisking constantly until it thickens. Simmer the sauce at least $^{1}/_{2}$ hour up to an hour, stirring frequently and skimming from time to time. Add the cream, if using. Season with the lemon juice, salt and pepper and boil again.

BROWN SAUCES

The most famous brown sauce, Espagnole, is made with a rich brown stock and a gently cooked brown roux. Although this rich sauce has a robust, yet fine, flavour, it is time-consuming and requires skill; a brown roux is tricky to make without scorching or separating. The sauce is intensified by adding fine (originally Spanish) ham and tomato paste, which adds to the glossy brown colour. Although it can be served by itself, it is also the base of many rich, dark French sauces such as demi-glaze, sauce Robert, and sauce Madere.

Nowadays, many cooks use a last minute thickener like arrowroot or potato starch, which produces a lighter sauce.

1 To make a basic brown sauce, bring 350ml (12 fl oz) rich brown stock to the boil over medium-high heat and reduce to about two-thirds its original volume. In a small cup, dissolve 1–2 teaspoons arrowroot or potato starch in 2 tablespoons Madeira or cold water. (The amount of starch depends on the thickness desired; dissolve the minimum, add half, then add more if required.)

2 Stir the paste, then stir into the boiling stock; the sauce will thicken immediately. If you like, stir in $1/2$ teaspoon tomato paste to enrich the colour. Simmer 2 minutes longer. Season with salt, if necessary, and pepper.

CLASSIC HOLLANDAISE

INGREDIENTS

3 egg yolks
3 tablespoons water
salt and cayenne or white pepper
175g (6oz) clarified unsalted butter
1–2 teaspoons lemon juice

1 In a small, heavy-based saucepan (non-aluminium), whisk the egg yolks, water, salt and pepper, until well-blended.

2 Set the saucepan over low heat and begin whisking vigorously and constantly until the mixture is thick and creamy and leaves a visible trail on the bottom of the pan. (Remove the pan from the heat occasionally to avoid overheating and curdling the egg yolks.)

3 Remove from the heat, and slowly and gradually whisk in the clarified butter, drop by drop. As the sauce thickens and absorbs the butter, begin pouring it in a very thin stream until the butter is incorporated (leaving any milky solids in the pan). Season with lemon juice and more salt and pepper if necessary.

BUSY COOKS

Both Hollandaise and Béarnaise can be made in a blender or food processor, in which case the egg yolks do not need heating; however, the clarified butter needs to be just about boiling.

1 Put the eggs, water, salt and pepper into the blender or food processor. Process 10 seconds, until light and foamy.

2 With the machine running, slowly and gradually pour the bubbling butter through the top of the feed tube, drop by drop, until the sauce thickens and absorbs the butter. Begin pouring it in a very thin stream until it is incorporated (leave any milky solids in the pan). Season as in step 3, Classic Hollandaise.

MEDITERRANEAN MARINADE

INGREDIENTS

450ml (15 fl oz) olive oil
250ml (8 fl oz) fresh lemon juice
150ml (5 fl oz) red wine vinegar
3 tablespoons chopped oregano
2 tablespoons minced garlic
1 teaspoon salt
1 teaspoon ground black pepper

Mix all ingredients except oil together. Blend until smooth in a food processor. Slowly add oil while blending. Cover and refrigerate until ready to use.

Use to marinate poultry, meat or seafood. It is a good idea to set a portion aside for basting during the cooking period.

BÉARNAISE SAUCE

Béarnaise is made in much the same way as Hollandaise, but a pungent reduction is made before adding the egg yolks and butter. The reduction should be reduced to about a tablespoon. Remove the pan from the heat occasionally while whisking (Step 2), to avoid overheating and curdling the egg yolks.

INGREDIENTS

3 tablespoons white wine vinegar
3 tablespoons dry white wine
10 peppercorns, lightly crushed
2–3 shallots, finely chopped
2 tablespoons fresh chopped
tarragon
1 tablespoon water
3 egg yolks
170g (6oz) clarified sweet butter
salt and white pepper

1 Put the vinegar, wine, peppercorns, shallots and 1 tablespoon chopped tarragon in a small, heavy-based saucepan. Bring to the boil over medium-high heat and simmer until reduced to a tablespoon of liquid. Remove from the heat and stir in a tablespoon cold water.

2 Add the egg yolks and season with salt and pepper, whisking to blend. Return to low heat and whisk vigorously and constantly, until the mixture is very thick and creamy and leaves a visible trail on the bottom of the pan.

3 Remove from the heat. Slowly and gradually whisk in the clarified butter, drop by drop. As the sauce thickens and absorbs the butter, begin pouring it in a very thin stream, until the butter is incorporated (leaving any milky solids in the pan).

4 If, by chance, the eggs have curdled, you may be able to save some of the sauce by straining it into a bowl. Stir in the remaining tarragon and adjust the seasoning.

WHITE BUTTER SAUCE (BEURRE BLANC): WHITE WINE BUTTER SAUCE

These fashionable, extremely rich and delicious sauces are more unstable than the classic emulsions because no egg yolks are used. The base is usually a reduction of wine, vinegar, stock or pan juices. To avoid separation, the butter must be very cold when it is beaten in so that it doesn't melt before it can be incorporated. Although this technique can be mastered, it is possible to "cheat". Adding a tablespoon of double cream or a teaspoon of cornflour to the reduction helps hold the emulsion and stabilize the sauce.

INGREDIENTS

3 tablespoons dry white wine
3 tablespoons white wine vinegar
2 shallots, finely chopped
1 tablespoon double cream or
    crème fraîche (optional)
250g (8oz) very cold unsalted
    butter, cut into small pieces
salt and white pepper

1 In a small heavy-based pan (not aluminium) bring the wine, vinegar and shallots to the boil. Boil until reduced to about 1 tablespoon. If using the cream, stir in and boil again until reduced.

2 Begin whisking in the butter over medium-high heat, piece by piece, until a smooth, creamy sauce begins to form. The French call this "mounting" the sauce with butter.

3 As the sauce emulsifies, add the butter 2–3 pieces at a time, whisking constantly over high heat until it just begins to boil and all the butter has been incorporated. Season and strain, if you like.

MAYONNAISE

This delicious sauce is used in salads, sandwiches and as part of other sauces.
It can be varied by using different oils, herbs and other flavourings.
Mayonnaise can also be made in a blender, food processor or with an electric mixer.
Make sure all the ingredients are at room temperature and, if making by hand, set the
bowl on a towel to keep it from sliding around.

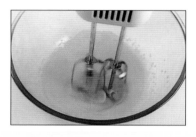

INGREDIENTS

2 egg yolks
2 tablespoons lemon juice or
white wine vinegar
1–2 tablespoons Dijon
mustard (optional)
salt and cayenne or white
pepper
350ml (12 fl oz) olive or
vegetable oil, or half of
each

1 To make mayonnaise, put the egg yolks,
half the lemon juice or vinegar, mustard and
salt and pepper into a bowl. Using a wire
whisk or electric mixer, beat until creamy
and well blended, about 1 minute. Begin
adding the oil slowly and gradually, drop by
drop, whisking constantly.

2 As the sauce begins to thicken, begin
pouring in the oil in a very slow steady
stream until all the oil is incorporated,
whisking constantly. Whisk in the remaining
lemon juice or vinegar and season, if
necessary. (If the sauce separates, slowly
whisk it into an egg yolk or 1 tablespoon of
Dijon mustard until it emulsifies.)

VINAIGRETTE

Vinaigrette is an unstable emulsion of vinegar and oil, Dijon mustard and seasonings. By whisking or shaking vigorously, the mustard helps to emulsify the oil and vinegar, but it will separate on standing or mixing with salad leaves or vegetables. Although the classic proportions are 3:1 oil to vinegar, the proportions will vary depending on the strength of the mustard and vinegar, so adjust to your taste. Add herbs, garlic and a little chopped shallot, if you like.

1 Put 2 tablespoons white or red wine vinegar or lemon juice into a small bowl. Whisk in a tablespoon of Dijon mustard and salt and pepper to taste.

2 Gradually whisk in 6–8 tablespoons of oil of your choice. Olive oil on its own may be too strong, so blend it with a good quality vegetable oil to your taste.

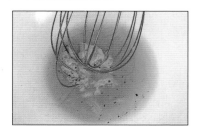

REMEMBER

Mayonnaise – as well as blender-made Béarnaise and Hollandaise – is made with raw egg yolks which can harbour *salmonella* bacteria. Pregnant women, children and the elderly should avoid undercooked or raw eggs.

Dairy Products and Eggs

Dairy foods and eggs form part of the foundation of Western cuisine. Consumed as foods in their own right, they are also the basis of soups, sauces, puddings, custards, batters, cakes, ice creams, toppings, mousses and many desserts. They are very nutritious, and are enduringly popular.

DAIRY PRODUCTS

MILK

Most milk and milk products consumed in the United Kingdom are produced from cows' milk, but goat, sheep and buffalo milk are appreciated in many parts of the world. Milk is the most basic of all foods and one of the first consumed by humans. Mothers' milk constitutes a complete diet, and cows' milk contains many nutrients, vitamins and calcium. Not only is it a popular beverage drunk on its own or flavoured, it also provides textures, flavour, colour and nutritional value to many cooked or prepared dishes.

Most milk is *pasteurized* to kill harmful bacteria and improve its keeping qualities. The milk is heated to 71°C (161°F) and kept at that temperature for 15 seconds. *Ultra-pasteurized* milk is heated to 135°C (275°F) for 2 to 4 seconds. This process destroys all bacteria and extends shelf life dramatically. UHT (*ultra-high temperature processing*) processes milk at an even higher temperature (138°–149°C/280°–300°F) for 2 to 6 seconds, so it can be stored without refrigeration for up to 3 months. Once opened, all processed milk should be treated like fresh milk and refrigerated. (Both milk and cream scorch easily when heated. Prevent this by first rinsing the pan with water. Then heat slowly, stirring occasionally.)

CREAM

Cream is the fatty portion of fresh milk which rises to the surface in a thick layer when milk is left to stand. Modern methods produce cream by centrifugal separator. The high-fat content gives cream a rich, buttery flavour and velvety texture. It is used to enrich soups and sauces, and to give body to puddings, custards and mousses. Added to baked goods and pastries, it provides extra richness and tenderness. Cream is used as a sauce in itself and is the basis for many ice creams and other frozen desserts.

Whipping cream Because of its high fat content, cream holds it shape when whipped. Whipped cream can be used as a garnish or added to mousses and parfaits to create other puddings or fillings. Whipped cream can be frozen, then defrosted just before using.

MILK GLOSSARY

Whole milk contains at least 3.9 per cent milk fat.

Semi-skimmed milk contains from 1.5 to 2 per cent milk fat. Increasingly popular because of current concerns about calories and fat.

Skimmed milk (fat-free milk). The fat content must be less than 0.1 per cent. Most skimmed milk is fortified with vitamins A and D.

Acidophilus milk is a cultured milk made from skimmed or low-fat milk. This helps maintain the balance of beneficial organisms in the intestines.

Evaporated milk is whole milk from which 60 per cent of the water has been removed. It is then canned and sterilized. Available as low fat (2 per cent) and skimmed, it can be reconstituted with an equal amount of water and used for cooking and drinking.

Condensed milk is similar to evaporated milk, but not usually heat-treated. Sweetened condensed milk contains 40–45 per cent sugar and is used in sweets and dessert recipes.

Powdered milk This is a completely dehydrated milk product which easily rehydrates in warm water. Instant powdered milk can be rehydrated in cold water and can be stored for long periods of time. (It is also available as whole-milk powder.) Powdered milk can be substituted for fresh in most recipes and is often used in breadmaking.

Homogenization is a process which disperses the fat globules evenly throughout the milk. Although most milk is homogenized, some dairies still sell unhomogenized milk.

CREAM GLOSSARY

Clotted cream A famous British speciality served with scones and jam, this yellowy cream with a solid butter-like texture contains over 55 per cent fat. It is made from unpasteurized milk left to allow the cream to rise to the surface. The cream is then heated so it sets and can be skimmed off and pasteurized.

Double cream contains at least 48 per cent milk fat. It whips quickly and holds its shape longer. It is used in the same way as whipping cream, but is richer and smoother.

Half cream Half cream and half milk, this product contains 12 per cent milk fat, and is also known as "coffee cream" or "top of the milk". It cannot be whipped, but can be used for a smooth, less rich substitute for cream in soups and sauces, or in coffee and on cereal.

Single cream contains 18 per cent butterfat. It cannot be whipped but is used in many sauces.

All cream, unless ultra-pasteurized (briefly heated to 149°C/300°F and then cooled), is highly perishable and should be kept in the coldest part of the refrigerator.

1 Pour whipping or double cream into a chilled bowl. Use a wire whisk or electric mixer to beat until cream begins to hold its shape. Beat into soft peaks when the whisk is lifted from the bowl.

2 For stiffly whipped cream, beat a little longer until stiffer peaks form and a clear trail is left in the cream. *Do not overbeat* or the cream will separate and become granular, eventually turning to butter.

CULTURED DAIRY PRODUCTS

Cultured dairy products have been used in many national cooking traditions to preserve milk. Adding a variety of bacterial cultures to milk or cream gives body and a unique tangy flavour.

TYPES OF CULTURED DAIRY PRODUCTS

Buttermilk Originally the remaining liquid residue from churning cream into butter. Today buttermilk is made by adding bacterial cultures to fresh pasteurized skimmed or semi-skimmed milk. This produces a tart, yet creamy-smooth product, drunk as a beverage or added to soups, pancakes, biscuits, cakes and tea breads.

Soured Cream Made by adding a bacterial culture to pasteurized, homogenized single cream, soured cream has a light, tangy flavour popular in many Eastern European dishes. A low-fat version is available. Soured cream will separate if boiled, so stir into hot sauces at the end of the cooking time, and heat gently just before serving.

Yogurt This popular product has been a fundamental food in the hot countries of the Middle East, Eastern Mediterranean and India for centuries. It has a thick, tart, custardy consistency. Greek-style yogurt, usually made with sheep's milk, is very popular in Britain and the Middle East. Yogurt, like soured cream, will curdle if boiled,

so treat as for sour cream.

Cottage Cheese The name "cottage" bears a true significance to this unripened soft cheese. For centuries farmers in Europe made this cheese in their cottages, and used the milk remaining after the cream had been skimmed off for buttermaking.

Some cottage cheese is produced by adding a bacterial culture to pasteurized skimmed milk or reconstituted non-fat dry milk. This bacterial culture forms lactic acid which coagulates the protein and causes the curd to form. Cottage cheese can also be made by adding acidifiers or the enzyme rennin to form the curd.

COOKING WITH YOGURT AND SOURED CREAM

Yogurt and soured cream can be added to soups, sauces and stews,
but handle it carefully.

1 Remove the simmering liquid from direct heat and whisk in small amounts of soured cream or yogurt. If sauce cools too much, reheat gently without simmering or boiling.

2 Alternatively, yogurt and soured cream can be stabilized by adding 2 teaspoons of cornflour per 225ml/8 fl oz before adding to sauces. Simmer, but do not boil vigorously or it will curdle.

COOKING WITH CRÈME FRAÎCHE

Crème fraîche was originally an unpasteurized cream which was left to sour naturally to develop a mellow, slightly nutty tang. Now produced commercially, it is made from pasteurized cream cultured with bacteria to replace those destroyed by pasteurization. It can contain as much as 60 per cent fat, although lower fat versions are available. If unavailable, it can be made at home (see below).

1 Stir together 450ml (16 fl oz) double cream (preferably *not* ultra-pasteurized) and 225ml (8 fl oz) buttermilk or soured cream. Heat to 29.5°C (85°F).

2 Pour into a container and cover loosely. Leave in a warm place 6 to 8 hours, until it is thickened and a nutty flavour develops. Stir, then cover, and refrigerate. Reserve 225ml (8 fl oz) to use as a starter for the next batch.

BUTTER AND MARGARINE

Butter is a solid fat made by churning cream; it contains about 80 per cent butterfat; and not more than 16 per cent water and whey (milk solids or proteins) left from the separating process. Salt was originally added to butter as a preservative, but is now used as a flavouring. Its flavour and richness are invaluable in cakes, pastries, biscuits and sauces, while it thickens and enriches soups, stews, casseroles and sauces. Butter is the basis of several classic sauces: Hollandaise, Béarnaise, and Beurre Blanc (white butter sauce). Flavoured butters can easily be made ahead and then used to garnish grilled or barbecued meats, poultry, fish and vegetables. Butter also adds flavour and an appetizing brown surface in frying and sautéeing.

Margarine was invented by a French chemist in 1869. A butter substitute, margarine is made from various vegetable oils, flavourings, colourings, emulsifiers, preservatives and vitamins. Composed of 80 per cent fat and 20 per cent water, it can be used instead of butter in most recipes, although butter must be used in certain pastries and sweets for satisfactory results. Do not substitute soft, diet or whipped margarines, which can contain up to 50 per cent water or air, in baking recipes or when frying.

COOKING WITH BUTTER

When butter is melted for pan frying, the butterfat separates from the water and whey (milk solids or proteins). In high heat or over a long time, the particles of whey will burn. Clarifying the butter allows the pure butterfat to be removed and used for sautéeing and frying at higher temperatures without burning. Clarified butter is also used for Hollandaise Sauce and as a dip for grilled or barbecued shellfish, asparagus and artichokes. Indian ghee is a type of clarified butter.

To make *brown butter* for fish or vegetables, slowly heat 115g (4oz) butter in a small heavy saucepan until golden and foaming and a strong nutty aroma is produced. Remove from the heat, add 1–2 tablespoons lemon juice and 1 tablespoon freshly chopped parsley, if you like. Pour over food while the butter is still bubbling. *Black butter* is cooked a little longer until very brown, when other ingredients can be added, and then served at once.

MAKING AND USING KNEADED BUTTER

Kneaded butter (*beurre manié*) is a paste made of equal amounts of butter and flour, used at the end of the cooking period to thicken and give richer consistency and flavour to sauces.

FLAVOURED BUTTERS

Flavoured butters can be made ahead and frozen, then used straight from the freezer. Soften 115g (4oz) butter, then flavour as follows:

Parsley butter Add 1 tablespoon lemon or lime juice, 2 tablespoons chopped parsley. Season with salt and pepper and serve over meat, fish, chicken or vegetables.

Herb butter Prepare as above but use tarragon, chives or coriander to replace parsley. Use to top meat, fish, chicken, vegetables, or in soups, stews and sauces.

Mustard butter Add 1 tablespoon Dijon or spicy brown mustard. Use with grilled or barbecued pork or lamb or in sandwiches.

Garlic butter Add 1–2 chopped or crushed garlic cloves. Use as a cooking medium or to make garlic bread.

Anchovy butter Add 2 tablespoons mashed anchovy fillets, 1 tablespoon lemon juice, and freshly ground black pepper. Use to top grilled or barbecued beef, lamb or fish, and as a base for canapés and sandwiches.

Sweet orange butter Add 1 tablespoon icing sugar, 1 tablespoon grated orange rind and juice. If you like, add 1 tablespoon orange liqueur. Use for hot desserts or muffins, pancakes and tea breads.

Honey butter Add 2–3 tablespoons honey and spread on bread, pancakes, waffles and tea breads.

Cinnamon butter Add 1–2 tablespoons icing sugar and $1/2$ teaspoon cinnamon. Use as honey butter.

Put the softened butter in a bowl and, using a wooden spoon or hand mixer, beat until soft and creamy. Add flavourings and seasonings and blend well.

CHEESE

Cheese is one of the oldest and most widely used foods. Eaten as a staple food, it is also used as an ingredient in many dishes. Cheese is made by coagulating heated whole, low-fat or skimmed milk with an enzyme, causing it to separate into curds and whey. The curds are pressed to form many kinds of cheese; whey is also used to make some cheese, such as ricotta or cottage cheese. Although most natural cheeses are high in fat, protein, calcium and many other minerals and vitamins, they also contain notable amounts of fat and salt.

COOKING WITH CHEESE

Cheese is generally used in four basic ways: as a flavouring, a topping, a filling or a dessert. Because of its high fat content, cheese can separate at high temperatures, becoming stringy and oily. When adding cheese to a sauce, remove the sauce from the heat and stir in the cheese until just melted. *For flavour* Use hard, aged cheeses which have a high fat content and intense flavour. Aged Parmesan is used to flavour pasta, risotto and soup; French Gruyère is used in soufflés, gratins, pastries and sauces; Mature English Cheddar can be substituted for Gruyère or blue cheeses used in salads, soups and sauces. *For filling* Many cheeses are used as fillings or part of fillings, to give extra flavour and body. Ricotta cheese is used in lasagna, feta cheese in Greek spanikopitas, ricotta and gorgonzola fill giant pasta shells. Cheeses are often baked whole, such as Brie in pastry, or breaded and fried. It is often a main ingredient in quiches and tarts. *For a topping* Soft or creamy cheeses melt easily and brown well. Mozzarella is often used as a topping for pizzas and many baked dishes, but Brie or Bel Paese could be used. Grated Gruyère is classic on French onion soup, as Cheddar is on Welsh Rarebit. Goat cheese can be grilled to use on salad or toast, or can top pizza instead of mozzarella. *Desserts* Most desserts use soft, mild fresh cheeses such as cream cheese for classic cheesecakes, coeur à la crème, cassata and pashka; Mascarpone, a rich Italian cream cheese, is used in tiramisu.

MACARONI AND CHEESE WITH BACON

This recipe uses a classic cheese sauce and a little crisp bacon for extra flavour, but it is just as good without it.

1 Put bacon into a small frying pan and set over medium-high heat. When bacon begins to cook, stir occasionally until it becomes crisp and golden. Using a slotted spoon, remove to a plate and set aside.

2 Add 15–25g (¹/₂–1oz) butter to the bacon fat and add breadcrumbs. Stir to coat and cook about 1 minute until just golden. Set aside.

3 Preheat the oven to 180°C (350°F 4/Gas). Melt remaining butter in a saucepan and add the onion; cook until softened. Stir in the flour and dry mustard. Cook for 2 minutes until a smooth roux forms.

INGREDIENTS
(Serves 4)

4 rashers bacon, sliced crossways
40–60g (1¹/₂–2oz) butter or margarine
90g (3oz) dry breadcrumbs
1 onion, chopped
1 tablespoon all purpose flour
1 teaspoon dry mustard
350ml (12 fl oz) milk
¹/₂ teaspoon salt
¹/₈ teaspoon cayenne pepper
225g (8oz) mature Cheddar cheese, grated
225g (8oz) elbow macaroni

4 Gradually stir in the milk and bring to the boil over medium heat. Stir constantly until thickened and smooth. Season with salt and cayenne pepper, remove from the heat, and stir in the cheese.

5 Cook the macaroni in a large pot of boiling salted water until tender. Drain and return to the pot. Stir in the cheese sauce and bacon. Pour into a baking dish, sprinkle the breadcrumbs over the top, and bake about 30 minutes until golden brown on top.

EGGS

Eggs, one of the most nutritious and versatile foods in the kitchen, are served on their own or used as an ingredient in everything from soups to desserts. Eggs provide texture, structure, flavour and moisture, as well as nutrition. Eggs can be brown or white; colour has no effect on quality or flavour, but depends on the breed of hen which lays it.

STORING EGGS

Eggs should be stored in the refrigerator in their carton to maintain maximum freshness and to avoid absorbing other food odours through their porous shells. Choose the freshest eggs for poaching or baking as they hold their shape best; when beating egg whites, choose older eggs, which whisk to a greater volume.

COOKING WITH EGGS

Eggs range in size from small to large, but most recipes use large eggs. Although eggs should be stored in the refrigerator, bring them to room temperature before cooking. Eggs are very sensitive to temperature: cold eggs can easily curdle a mayonnaise or cake batter; room-temperature or warm egg whites will whisk to a greater volume. Eggs will continue to cook if left in a hot pan or on a hot plate, so transfer to a serving plate immediately. Use moderate heat for cooking most egg dishes, except omelettes.

SHELLING MEDIUM- OR HARD-COOKED EGGS

Very fresh eggs are harder to shell than slightly older ones: plunging the cooked eggs into very cold water as soon as they are cooked helps loosen the shell.

1 Crack the egg around its centre, as for separating the egg. Gently roll egg on a work surface until the eggshell is cracked all around the middle.

2 Peel the eggshell away from the white. Holding the egg under cold running water helps the shell come away. Dry gently before using. Store peeled eggs in salted water.

SEPARATING EGGS

The best way to separate the yolk from the white is by using the shell. Avoid breaking the egg into one hand and allowing the white to run through the fingers while cupping the yolk. The white can absorb grease and odours which will inhibit its beating qualities.

1 Have two bowls ready. Crack the egg as close to its middle as possible by hitting the shell firmly against the edge of a bowl or sharp edge of a counter. Using your thumbs, pull shells apart, allowing some of the white to fall into the bowl.

2 Pour yolk from shell to shell, allowing white to dribble into the bowl. Use one side of the shell to detach remaining white from yolk. Use a shell half to remove any bits of yolk which might slip into whites.

3 Place yolk gently into the second bowl.

Some eggs contain the salmonella bacteria, which is killed by long or high heat. Small babies, young children, pregnant women and the elderly should avoid softly cooked eggs and dishes which might contain under-cooked or raw eggs, such as mousses, soufflés, soft meringues, mayonnaise and so on.

WHISKING EGG WHITES

Beaten egg whites are the basis for meringues and are used to lighten soufflés and mousses. The whites must be free of any traces of egg yolk, oil from hands or bowls and even water. A pinch of salt or cream of tartare added at the start of the beating will help them stiffen. Sugar stabilizes beaten whites and prevents them from becoming grainy, but must be added after the whites are stiff. Do not overwhisk or they will be too stiff to fold into the base mixture. Use a copper or stainless steel bowl, as glass and ceramic bowls seem to "repel" the whites and separate them. Plastic can harbour traces of grease or oil, so avoid using it. If in doubt, rinse the bowl with vinegar or lemon juice to remove any impurities, then rinse and dry.

1 Put whites in a large, grease-free bowl, preferably copper or stainless steel. Begin beating with a large balloon whisk or electric mixer until the whites are "broken" and foamy. If not using a copper bowl, add $1/4$ teaspoon cream of tartare or a pinch of salt to stabilize the whites.

2 Increase speed and continue beating until whites hold soft peaks when the whisk or beaters are lifted from the bowl.

3 For meringues, add about three-quarters of the measured sugar, 1 tablespoon at a time, beating well until the sugar is dissolved (rub a little meringue between thumb and finger – if it is gritty, continue beating). Continue until whites are stiff and glossy.

4 Sprinkle on remaining sugar and gently fold into the meringue. Use as directed.

WHISKING EGG YOLKS

Egg yolks are often whisked separately with or without sugar, sometimes over heat. The whisking increases volume and lightens sauces such as Hollandaise (page 42) or adds air for cakes or batters.

Rinse a bowl with warm water, then dry it. Add yolks and sugar, if directed, and whisk by hand or with an electric mixer until yolks become light in colour, thick and moussy.

FOLDING EGG WHITES

Folding is one of the most important cooking techniques. Because beaten egg whites contain so much air, they are difficult to add to a heavier mixture without losing volume. Folding is a method of combining a light mixture and a heavier one without deflating the lighter mixture.

1 Do not overbeat egg whites or they will not mix in smoothly and will deflate. To "lighten" the heavier or base mixture, add about a quarter of the beaten whites, and stir them in thoroughly.

2 Spoon in remaining whites and gently fold in, using a rubber spatula or metal spoon. Cut down into the centre of the mixture to the bottom, scooping under and up along one side of the bowl, turning it as you go.

Or, turn the lightened base mixture onto remaining beaten whites. Fold in lightly,

cutting down the centre with the spatula to the bottom of the bowl, then turning and rolling the mixture over onto itself.

BOILING EGGS

Whatever method you prefer, eggs should never be boiled, but gently simmered. To avoid cracking, eggs should be at room temperature. They can be soft-cooked (soft white and yolk), medium (firm white and soft yolk), or hard-cooked (firm white and yolk). Plunge into cold water immediately after cooking time is completed to prevent a greenish-grey ring around the yolk. Hard-boiled eggs can be refrigerated in their shells up to a week.

FOR SOFT- OR HARD-COOKED EGGS:
Fill a medium saucepan with enough salted water to cover eggs; bring to a rolling boil. Gently lower eggs into water. Simmer. For soft-cooked eggs, cook 3–5 minutes or to taste. For medium, 5–7 minutes, and for hard-cooked, 10–12 minutes.

TO CODDLE EGGS:
Put eggs in a saucepan and cover with cold water. Bring to a boil and remove from heat. Cover and allow to stand 6–8 minutes for a soft egg, 8–10 minutes for a hard egg, or to taste. Remove from the water and serve immediately or plunge into ice water and cool. Peel as soon as eggs are cool. This method produces a medium- or hard-cooked egg with a more tender white; it is often used for eggs for Caesar salad and eggs to be set in moulded dishes.

POACHING EGGS

Poached eggs are cooked in just simmering water to produce a moist egg with firm white enclosing a soft yolk. Use the freshest eggs possible; the fresher the egg, the closer the white clings, producing a neat, firm shape. Older eggs will disintegrate as soon as they hit the water. A little vinegar in the water helps the white coagulate. Poached eggs are served on toast for breakfast, in Eggs Florentine, Eggs Benedict and in many other dishes.

1 Begin by cooking 1 or 2 eggs at a time. Fill a deep skillet or wide saucepan with 7.5cm (3in) water. If you like, add 2 tablespoons vinegar to 1 litre (1 pints) water. Bring to the boil. Break egg into a saucer or small dish. Using a wooden spoon, stir the water vigorously to form a vortex. Quickly slide the egg into the vortex; this will help shape the egg. Continue stirring and sliding in the eggs. The more experienced you become, the more eggs you will be able to handle.

2 Reduce the heat and poach in the just-simmering water 3–4 minutes or to taste. Lift egg out using a slotted spoon, and press gently with a finger. It should feel just slightly firm. Remove to kitchen paper to drain slightly.

BAKED EGGS

Producing what are sometimes called "shirred eggs," is an easy technique to master. Adding extra flavourings or a more elaborate base, such as creamed leeks with smoked salmon, produces an elegant appetizer for a dinner party or a simple lunch or supper.

1 Butter four ramekins. Sprinkle the bottom with salt and pepper. Break 1 egg into each ramekin and, if you like, pour 1 tablespoon of cream over each egg, or dot with a little butter.

BAKED EGGS CONTINUED

2 Cover loosely with foil. Set into a deep fryng pan or small flameproof casserole. Fill with boiling water. Cook gently on top of the stove or bake in a 190°C (375°F/Gas 5) oven 5–6 minutes until the white is just set and the yolk still soft. Jiggle one of the ramekins to test the set. Remove from water bath; remember eggs will continue cooking in the dish. Serve immediately.

3 Alternatively, butter 4 individual baking dishes. Spread a prepared base on the bottom (creamed leeks, chopped tomatoes or spring onions). Make a well in the centre of each and break an egg into it. Add a little cream or dot with butter, and cover loosely. Bake as above 10–12 minutes, until lightly set.

SCRAMBLED EGGS

In France, good scrambled eggs are considered an art; gently stirred over low heat to a thick creamy purée, they make an elegant dish garnished with truffles, smoked salmon or chopped chives. They make a delicious topping for tender pastry, tartlets or toast. Purists do not add water or milk before cooking, saying it can cause sticking, but it is a question of taste. A spoonful of thick cream or *crème fraîche* at the end of cooking lowers the temperature and stops the cooking, not to mention adding a delicious richness.

1 Break 2 or 3 eggs per person into a bowl. Season with salt and pepper, and beat until well blended. Melt 1–2 tablespoons butter over medium-low heat in a heavy saucepan or deep frying pan. Add the eggs and cook gently, stirring constantly with a wooden spoon.

2 Continue stirring as the eggs thicken, until they are soft set and creamy. Remove from the heat and stir until the desired consistency is reached – the heat of the pan will continue to cook them. Alternatively, cook slightly longer over the heat, stir in a knob of cold butter or spoonful of cream, then serve.

FRIED EGGS

Fried eggs are often served with crisp bacon or sausages. The fried egg is the centrepiece of the great British breakfast, surrounded by bacon, sausages, mushrooms, baked beans, black pudding and fried bread. Butter, oil, bacon or other dripping can be used for cooking.

1 Melt 15–25g ($^1/_2$–1oz) of fat in a heavy-based frying pan over medium heat. When fat is sizzling, break in 2 eggs.

2 Fry 1–2 minutes, basting with fat, until white is firm and begins to crisp around the edge. The yolk should be soft.

3 For "over easy" eggs, use a spatula to flip each egg carefully. Cook 15 seconds longer, then serve. Alternatively, when whites are just set, add 1–2 tablespoons water to the pan. Cover and cook 2–3 minutes, until done to your taste.

MAKING AN OMELETTE

Omelettes can be rolled or folded, or they can be made flat. They can be filled with a variety of ingredients and make a tasty breakfast, lunch or supper. A well-seasoned omelette pan is essential, although the newer nonstick pans are excellent. For a 2–3 egg omelette for one person, a 17.5–20cm (7–8-in) pan is just the right size; 4–5 eggs for two people will cook better in a 22.5cm (9in) pan.

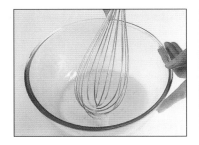

1 Break 2 to 3 eggs into a bowl, season with salt and pepper, and beat until well-blended in a heavy-based omelette pan, melt 1–2 tablespoons butter over medium-high heat, tilting pan to coat well with butter.

2 When butter is hot and foaming and just beginning to brown, pour in eggs, shaking pan to distribute egg mixture evenly. Cook about 10 seconds, until the bottom begins to set.

3 Using a metal spatula or fork, gently pull setting egg mixture from the edge of pan to centre, tilting pan so that the uncooked egg flows onto the pan base and side. Continue pulling in from the edge until most of the egg is set but the top is still moist and creamy.

4 Sprinkle 1 tablespoon chopped fresh parsley or chives over the center, then sprinkle with 2–3 tablespoons grated Cheddar or other cheese. Run spatula around the edge of pan to loosen omelette from the edge. Tilt pan and fold top third of the omelette over onto the centre.

5 Hold pan over a warmed plate and begin to slide the lower third of the omelette onto the plate.

6 Tip pan over to help omelet fold itself, so that the omelette rolls onto the plate with the edges neatly folded under. If you like, brush the surface with a little melted butter and sprinkle with a few herbs. Serve immediately.

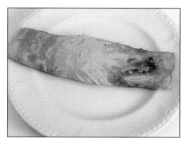

7 Alternatively, for a slightly easier method, proceed as in Step 5 but fold the omelette in half instead of thirds, then slide onto a warmed plate. Finish as in Step 6.

CRÊPES AND SOUFFLÉS

Batters are a mixture of flour, liquid (this can vary from milk or water to cream or even beer) and eggs. The proportions differ, depending on its ultimate texture. Batters can be sweet, as for pancakes or waffles, or savoury as for Yorkshire puddings, popovers or blini. They can be thick for fritters and for coating foods like fish, or thin for popovers and delicate crêpes.

MAKING A SOUFFLÉ

The soufflé is a great example of the egg as a binding and leavening agent. The yolks go into a basic sauce mixture, then the whites are beaten until stiff and light. They are then folded into the basic mixture, and the result baked to a puffy golden brown. Soufflés can be sweet or savoury, hot or cold, although the last is not a true soufflé, but more a mousse set with gelatine, presented in the style of a soufflé. All soufflés depend on two techniques; properly beaten egg whites carefully folded into the base mixture, and proper preparation of the dish.

BUSY COOKS

Crêpe and other batters can be made in a food processor or blender. Put the sifted flour, sugar and salt into the bowl of the food processor fitted with the metal blade. Add the eggs and 225ml (8 fl oz) of the liquid and process 30–40 seconds until well blended. Strain into a measuring cup and stir in the butter. Allow to stand at least 1/2 hour, then add more liquid if necessary.

MAKING CRÊPES: FRENCH STYLE

Crêpes are popular and versatile. They can be filled with sweet or savoury mixtures, folded and heated in sauce, or eaten freshly made with a dusting of sugar and a squeeze of lemon juice, as they are eaten on street corners in France. Allowing the batter to stand lets the gluten in the flour relax and allows the maximum liquid to be absorbed. For this reason, a little milk or liquid is often added before cooking to thin the batter to the desired consistency. A non-stick pan makes greasing in between each crêpe unnecessary.

INGREDIENTS

(makes about 18 crêpes)

150g (5oz) plain flour
$^1/_8$ teaspoon salt
1–2 teaspoons sugar
3 eggs
300ml (10 fl oz) milk or half milk
and half water
50–65g (2–2$^1/_2$oz) melted butter

1 Sift flour, salt, and sugar into a large bowl. In another bowl, beat eggs with 225ml (8 fl oz) of the liquid. Make a well in the centre of the flour mixture and gradually whisk in egg mixture.

2 Draw in the flour from the side of the well to form a smooth batter the consistency of whipping cream.

3 Strain into a large measuring jug.

4 Stir in the butter until blended. Allow to stand $^1/_2$ hour or overnight, refrigerated. If the batter becomes too thick, thin with a little milk or water.

5 Heat the crêpe pan over medium heat. Brush or spray lightly with a little melted butter or oil. Pour 3–4 tablespoons of batter onto the pan, tilting and turning the pan to spread batter thinly and evenly; pour off any excess or fill in any holes, if you like.

FRENCH-STYLE CRÊPES CONTINUED

6 Cook about 1 minute until golden brown. Using a metal spatula, loosen the edges of the crêpe and shake pan to make sure it is not stuck.

7 Slide the spatula under and flip the pancake.

8 Cook 20–30 seconds longer, then slide out onto a plate. Continue with remaining batter, greasing the pan between each crêpe, or as necessary.

9 If using crêpes immediately, stack directly onto each other. To store for later use, put a sheet of wax paper or cling film between each crêpe as you make them. Leave to cool then wrap well, and refrigerate or freeze until needed.

PREPARING A SOUFFLÉ DISH

The straight-sided ceramic dish is considered classic, since the vertical, fluted sides guide the soufflé upward, but any ovenproof dish will do. Use melted or very soft butter or oil and a pastry brush to coat the dish. Then refrigerate and, when set, butter it again. Some recipes specify coating the buttered dish with breadcrumbs, cheese or sugar.

CHEESE SOUFFLÉ

1 Prepare a 1.2–1.3 litre (2–2¹/₄ pint) soufflé dish and set aside. Make a medium white sauce (page 38), reduce heat, and beat in yolks, one at a time, beating well after each addition. Cook, stirring constantly, about 2 minutes, until the mixture thickens slightly. Remove from heat and stir in cheeses, mustard and nutmeg. Set aside and keep warm, stirring occasionally to prevent a skin from forming.

INGREDIENTS

(Serves 4–6)

225ml (8 fl oz) medium white sauce
4 eggs, separated
1 tablespoon Dijon mustard
freshly grated nutmeg
90g (3oz) grated sharp Cheddar or
    Monterey Jack cheese
1–2 tablespoons freshly grated
    Parmesan cheese
1 egg white

2 Preheat oven to 190°C (375°F/Gas 5). Set a baking sheet on a rack in the lower third of the oven (this helps set the bottom of the soufflé). Beat all 5 egg whites until just stiff. *Do not overbeat.* (In a sweet soufflé, sugar would be added in this step.)

3 Stir a large spoonful of beaten whites into the warm cheese base. Using a rubber spatula or large metal spoon, lightly fold in remaining whites until just blended. *Do not overfold* or you will deflate the mixture.

4 Spoon mixture into the dish and gently smooth the top. Tap firmly on your work surface to dislodge any large bubbles.

5 Bake about 30 minutes, until risen and golden. Shake dish; the soufflé should just tremble, indicating it is still soft in the centre. Cook 5 minutes longer for a firm soufflé. Serve immediately. Alternatively, bake in a 200°C (400°F/Gas 6) oven for 5 minutes, then reduce heat to 180°C (350°F/Gas 4), and cook 20–25 minutes longer.

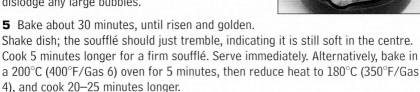

CUSTARD

Custard is a mixture of eggs, milk, sugar (if it is to be sweet rather than savoury) and flavourings. There are two types of custard: *stirred custard*, cooked over heat while stirring until thickened, and *set custard*, slowly baked in the oven in a *bain marie* or water bath.

Custards can be temperamental; the most important aspect of cooking is the heat. Custard thickens because the proteins in the egg coagulate when heated. If heated too hot or too quickly, custards will curdle, separate, and start to scramble. Always cook custard *slowly* over gentle heat. Use a double boiler or bowl set over a pan of hot, not boiling water. The custard should thicken slowly; you can feel the consistency on the bottom of the pan. Custard is cooked when the thickened mixture coats the back of a wooden spoon and a clear track remains when a finger is drawn through it. If custard begins to curdle, remove from the heat and beat, or whisk in an ice cube to lower the temperature.

Stirred custard, Crème anglaise, or custard sauce is used hot or cold as a sauce for many desserts, as a filling for pastry, and as a base for ice creams, mousses and many other desserts. It will thicken at 180°C (350°F) and takes at least 10–12 minutes.

Baked custard needs to cook gently in a moderate oven in a *bain marie* – water bath – which insulates it from direct heat and protects against overheating.

Crème caramel or flan is probably the most famous set custard. Like a soufflé, when done its centre should jiggle slightly, and a knife inserted halfway between the centre and edge comes out clean. Set custards are the basis of many quiches and tarts. As a general rule, 1 whole egg or 2 egg yolks will thicken 225ml (8 fl oz) of milk. The mixture can be made richer by using more yolks or cream instead of milk.

CUSTARD SAUCE

In Britain, Custard Sauce is the traditional topping for many fruit desserts and puddings. A little cornflour or custard powder is stirred into the beaten egg mixture before adding the milk, stabilizing the yolks and allowing the mixture to be brought to a boil; use about 1 teaspoon per 225ml (8 fl oz) of milk.

STIRRED CUSTARD (CUSTARD SAUCE)

1 Split the vanilla pod and scrape seeds into a heavy-based saucepan; add the pod.

INGREDIENTS

450ml (16 fl oz) milk
1 vanilla pod or 1¹/₂ teaspoons vanilla
   essence
4 egg yolks
3 tablespoons sugar

2 Pour in milk and bring to a simmer. Remove from heat, cover, and allow to infuse about 15 minutes. Strain.

3 In a medium bowl, beat egg yolks with sugar until lightened and thickened, about 3 minutes. Slowly pour in warm milk, whisking until well blended.

4 Return mixture to saucepan or top of a double boiler or bowl set over a pan of just-simmering water. Cook over low heat, stirring constantly, until mixture thickens and coats the back of a wooden spoon, leaving a clear trail when a finger is drawn through it. This will take at least 10 minutes.

5 Immediately strain into a cold bowl, set over ice or ice water. Stir in vanilla essence, if using, and stir custard until it cools slightly. Custard can be served hot or chilled. Cover with cling film to prevent a skin from forming if serving cold.

FISH AND SHELLFISH

Fish are featuring ever more strongly in our daily diet. Bolstered by a strong press extolling its healthful qualities — generally low in fat, and high in protein, vitamins and minerals — it is the perfect food for today's demanding eaters. While white fish is the lowest in calories and thus the choice of dieters, oily fish can help in the fight against heart disease.

FISH

There are hundreds of species of fish: saltwater fish from the oceans and freshwater fish from lakes, rivers and streams. Most fish fall into two main categories, depending on their skeletal structure: round fish and flat fish. Round fish generally have plump, thick bodies which can be divided into equal fillets or cut crosswise into steaks or cutlets. These fish tend to have secondary bones which run through the fillets and require removal before cooking. Flat fish, such as plaice, have a flat central bone with rows of bones along each side. This structure yields 4 fillets and, although they are easy to fillet, the fillets are not of equal size, the top ones generally being larger.

Very large round fish, like tuna and swordfish, have a large, central, bony spine with four rows of bones radiating out, dividing the fish into quarters. These fish are generally cut crossways into large steaks which are boneless when separated from the main structure.

The fat content of fish helps determine the most suitable cooking method. Lean fish have firm white flesh and a mild flavour with less than 5 per cent fat. Sole, plaice, halibut, snapper, sea bass, turbot and cod are examples of lean fish which dry out easily. Cooking methods such as steaming, poaching, baking in a sauce or paper, battering or coating before frying are most suitable. Salmon, mackerel, herring and carp are the oiliest fish, followed by tuna, swordfish, trout, mullet and monkfish. Oily fish contain 5–50 per cent fat, so they are ideal for baking, grilling, pan frying, or barbecuing.

COOKING FISH

Fish can be cooked by many methods. It can be poached, steamed, pan or deep-fried, grilled, barbecued or baked. It can be used in fillings, mousses, pâtés and terrines. Whatever method you choose, fish cooks quickly, so do not overcook or the flesh will become dry and lose flavour. Raw fish is translucent and becomes opaque when cooked.

CHOOSING AND STORING FISH

Choose the freshest possible fish from a reliable fish market or a supermarket with a rapid turnover. When buying frozen fish, select the best quality with all the packaging intact and no signs of ice or blood. Thaw frozen fish in a container overnight in the refrigerator, although fillets and steaks can be cooked frozen. If cooking frozen fish, add a few minutes to the cooking time.

Fresh fish should have a mild, sweet odour and firm, resilient flesh that springs back when touched. The eyes should protrude, not be sunken; the gills should be bright red or pink, not brownish; and scales should be shiny and bright. Fish fillets or steaks should look fresh and moist, not dry, although it's best to buy portions which are prepared at your request.

Fish deteriorates quickly, so keep it in the coldest part of your refrigerator for as short a time as possible. Whole fish keep longer than fillets, and lean fish keep better than oily fish. Arrange dried fillets or steaks in a kitchen-paper-lined dish and cover tightly with cling film. Set over ice in a larger dish, if possible.

PREPARING WHOLE FISH

Most fish have scales which must be removed before cooking. Although a professional will scale and clean a fish for you, it is an easy skill to master.

IF COOKING A ROUND FISH WHOLE:
The fins may be left on to help keep the shape, or just trimmed. Using kitchen scissors or a sharp knife, make a cut along both sides of the dorsal (back) and anal fins, then pull the fin toward the fish head to remove it; snip any smaller fins. Trim off fins behind the gills.

TRIMMING THE TAIL:
With the scissors trim the tail into a "V" shape for a neat presentation.

TO SCALE ROUND FISH:
Salt your hands for a better grip or hold the tail firmly with some folded kitchen paper. Put the fish on a board in a deep sink and, using a fish scaler or back of a large knife, scrape the scales off, working from the tail towards the head. Turn the fish over and scale the other side; rinse the fish and the board.

TO CLEAN AND GUT A ROUND FISH:
Use a sharp knife to slit the underside (belly) from the gills to the rear vent (anal fin). Do not insert the knife too far or it may pierce the stomach. (The head may be cut off before gutting if you wish.) Carefully pull out the stomach contents.

REMOVE THE GILLS:
Do this either by hooking a finger around them and pulling, or by cutting them out. Rinse the cavity well then, using a teaspoon, scrape along the vertebral column to remove the black blood or kidney. Rinse again and dry well.

PREPARING WHOLE FISH CONTINUED

FLAT FISH:
To trim, use kitchen scissors to trim off most of the fins.

To clean, make a small slit behind the gills and pull out the stomach, then rinse. Alternatively cut off the head by making a "V" shaped cut around it, then pulling the head away and removing the stomach and viscera.

SKINNING FISH FILLETS

Some fish have very tough or oily skins, which should be removed before poaching, steaming, deep frying or pan frying. Most fish skin can be removed with a knife, but catfish, monkfish, sole and others are best skinned before filleting. Skinning fillets is quick and simple; skinning whole fish may require the assistance of a professional.

TO SKIN FISH FILLETS:
1 Place on a work surface skin-side down, with the tail end towards you. Make a small crosswise cut down to the skin at the top of the tail.

2 Grip the tail end of the skin and lay the knife against the skin with the blade almost parallel to it. Using a gentle sawing motion, work the knife away from you, separating the skin from the flesh.

BONING FISH

Both round and flat fish can be boned and stuffed for an elegant party presentation. In both cases, the head can be left on or taken off, but the fish should be cleaned. If the fish is to be stuffed through the back, it must be cleaned through the gills.

1 Holding the cavity open, slide filleting knife between rib cage bones and flesh, cutting them loose from the belly edge, working up along the bones to the backbone.

2 Turn fish onto its belly, opening the flaps like an overturned book. Press along the spine to loosen bone from flesh.

3 With scissors, cut through the backbone at the tail and head end (if the head remains) and peel it off the flesh, pulling any attached bones with it. Open fish out flat and remove any small pin bones, as for the fillets. The fish is ready for use.

CUTTING FILLETS AND STEAKS

Buying a whole fish can often be more economical than buying fillets or steaks. Removing the bones yourself is easy work with a sharp filleting knife, one with a long, thin, flexible blade. Keep the bones and trimmings (not the skin) of lean fish for making stock (page 35).

Round fish yield two long fillets, one from each side. Flat fish yield four fillets, two slightly thicker fillets from the top and two from the bottom. The fish should be scaled before filleting if it is to be cooked with skin.

TO FILLET A ROUND FISH:
1 Put fish on a board or work surface and cut off the head just behind the gills.

2 Holding knife parallel to the backbone and beginning at the top end, cut through skin and into the flesh. Cut along backbone to the tail, holding the knife against the bone. You will feel the knife cutting through the secondary pin bones. Turn fish over and repeat with the other side.

3 Trim any remaining bones from fillets. Use tweezers to pull out the little pin bones, feeling along the length of the fillet with your fingers.

TO FILLET A FLAT FISH:
1 Make a curved cut behind the head or cut it off completely. Using the tip of the knife, cut around the outside edge of the fish to outline the two fillets; cut crossways across the tail.

2 Locate the centre spine. Cut a straight line from head to tail along it. Holding the knife flat against the bones, cut away the fillet using short strokes and pressing against the bone. Turn fish around and repeat.

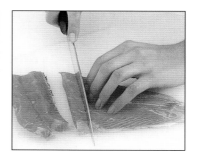

LARGE FILLETS:
Fillets from a salmon, bass or other fish can be cut into scallops about 1cm ($^1/_2$ in) thick for an attractive presentation and quicker cooking. Working towards the tail and holding the knife parallel to the fillet, cut thin, even, diagonal slices.

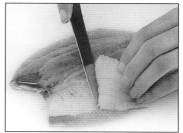

TO CUT STEAKS FROM A ROUND FISH:
Use a large heavy knife to slice the fish crosswise into steaks between 2.5–4cm (1–1$^1/_2$ in) thick. The larger centre slices are called cutlets. The tail section is too small for steaks but can be divided horizontally to make two fillets.

POACHING FISH

Poaching is a gentle method of cooking in liquid, which adds moisture and flavour to whole fish as well as smaller fillets, steaks or cutlets. The poaching liquid – fish stock (page 35), a *court bouillon* (page 31), plain water or wine – can be used to make the accompanying sauce. Fish can be poached on top of the stove or in the oven.

1 To poach a large fish, prepare the poaching liquid and cool completely; use to fill the fish pan or a large casserole. Put the fish on the rack, or set on a long double layer of muslin.

2 Lower fish into the liquid (if using muslin, tie the ends to the handles). Add extra water, if necessary. Bring to the boil over medium-high heat, cover and simmer gently until done. Drain well and keep warm, if serving hot. Cool, then refrigerate if serving cold.

3 To oven-poach smaller fish, fillets or steaks, place them in a greased oven-proof dish. Pour in enough poaching liquid to cover. Cover the dish with a piece of greased paper or foil.
4 Bring the liquid to the boil over medium heat, then transfer the baking dish to 180°C (350°F/Gas 4) oven and poach until the fish tests done. Remove from the liquid to serve hot. To serve cold, remove from the oven just before the fish tests done, as it will continue to cook in its liquid.

TESTING TO SEE IF IT IS COOKED

1 Make a small slit in the thickest part of a whole fish, lifting gently with the blade of a knife. The fish is cooked when the flesh is opaque and pulls away from the bone easily. A large fish will continue cooking when removed from the heat, so if the flesh is slightly opaque near the bone, it will finish cooking on standing.

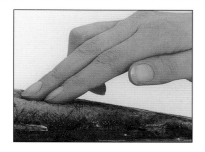

2 The flesh of cooked fish will feel firm to the touch and offer a little resistance. Raw fish will feel soft, almost mushy.

3 Fish is perfectly cooked when the flesh *just* begins to separate into flakes. If it flakes easily, it will be overdone and dry.

CANADIAN DEPARTMENT OF FISHERIES METHOD

This standard method for timing poached fish is a useful guide.

1 Measure the fish at its thickest point. For each 2.5cm (1in) of thickness, allow 10 minutes cooking time (20 minutes if the fish is frozen).

2 When testing, if the fish is very thick, remove it from its liquid. Rest the rack across the pan. Slide a sharp knife blade into the back of the fish near the dorsal fin. The flesh should look opaque and will not cling to the bones.

STEAMING FISH

Steaming fish is a simple moist-heat method, favoured by the Chinese and those wishing to avoid cooking with fat. Steaming takes about the same time as poaching, but only a small amount of liquid is needed. The liquid should be boiling when the fish is set over it. A very light spray or coating of oil on the steamer rack will keep the fish from sticking.

1 Arrange fish steaks, cutlets, fillets or small whole fish on the steamer rack and set over boiling water. Steam, covered, until fish tests done.

2 Put fish on a plate and set it at the bottom of a bamboo steamer. Place over a saucepan filled with simmering water.

3 Fish can be steamed on a plate without a steamer. Put a small rack, ramekin, or upside down bowl in the bottom of a wok. Fill wok with 5cm (2in) boiling water. Set plate on bowl and steam as above.

4 Larger fish or fillets can be steamed on a plate or piece of heavy-duty foil set in a roasting pan of boiling water. Cover pan tightly with foil and steam on stop of stove or in the oven as above.

PAN- AND DEEP-FRYING

Both pan-frying and deep-frying are excellent ways of cooking fish. Pan-frying uses a shallow layer of fat in a frying pan, while deep-frying requires a deep-fryer, saucepan or wok filled with 7.5–10cm (3–4in) or more of oil. Both methods use high heat, which seals in the moisture and flavour of the fish. In these methods the fish is usually coated with crumbs or batter.

TO PAN FRY FISH:

1 Heat just enough clarified butter (page 39) or a mixture of butter and oil to cover the bottom of the pan evenly, over medium-high heat.

2 When the fat is very hot but not smoking, add fish in a single layer. Cook about 2 minutes per side (depending on the thickness), until golden brown. Drain on kitchen paper before serving.

TO DEEP-FRY FISH:

1 Fill a deep-fryer, deep saucepan, or wok with 7.5–10cm (3–4in) oil. Heat to 190°C (375°F) and carefully put in the fish. Do not put too many pieces in at one time; this lowers the temperature of the oil.

2 Fry until crisp and golden, turning once. Remove with slotted spoon. Drain on kitchen paper.

SERVING A WHOLE FISH

A whole poached fish is best skinned before presentation. The fish should be skinned while still warm or the skin will be difficult to remove. Grilled or barbecued fish can be served with its crisp skin.

COATING FISH FOR FRYING

A coating can protect the delicate flesh of fish, keeping in moisture and flavour. Coatings are usually made of breadcrumbs, cornmeal or even oatmeal, or of a batter of flour and egg. Batter coatings are usually used in deep-frying.

BREADCRUMBS:
1 To coat fillets, steaks, or small whole fish: dry fish pieces well and season with salt and pepper. Put flour in a shallow plate and season. Finally put bread crumbs (dried or fresh), in another shallow bowl. Beat 1–2 eggs (depending on quantity) in another bowl. Season. Set aside.

2 Dip fish pieces (one at a time) first into the flour, turning to coat lightly and shaking off any excess. Then dip the floured fish into the beaten egg, turning to coat all sides.

3 Dip the egged pieces into the crumbs, pressing to help them adhere, turning and coating on all sides. Gently shake off any excess. Arrange on a plate or baking sheet and refrigerate at least 15 minutes before frying; this helps set the coating.

TO BATTER-COAT FISH:
Prepare batter and allow to rest as recipe directs. Dry fish or pieces very well and dust very lightly with flour. Using tongs or fingers, dip one piece at a time into the batter, coating completely. Then immediately lower the fish gently into the hot fat.

GRILLING AND BARBECUING FISH

Grilling is an intense dry-heat method which is best suited to oily fish such as salmon, tuna, trout or swordfish. Marinating fish adds moisture.
Barbecuing adds a wonderful outdoor flavour to fresh fish. Strongly flavoured, oily varieties barbecue best. Fish can be barbecued whole or cut into cubes and skewered. Whole fish should be scored to prevent curling and ensure even cooking.

1 Use a sharp knife to make 3–4 diagonal slashes on each side, about 0.5–1cm ($^1/_4$–$^1/_2$in) deep. This allows heat to penetrate more quickly. The skin of large fish steaks can be snipped at the back to help prevent curling.

2 Dry fish well and season as recipe directs. If fish has been marinating, drain well. Place on the grill pan lined with foil, and brush with butter, oil or any remaining marinade.

3 Grill 2cm ($^3/_4$ in) thick buttered or oiled steaks or fillets 7.5–10cm (3–4in) from the heat, basting and turning as recipe directs, until done. Barbecue on the grill over medium coals 4–5 minutes, depending on thickness, turning once, until done.

4 To grill leaner fish, add a little liquid to the pan (stock, water, wine, etc.) to provide extra moisture. Baste once or twice to keep fish moist.

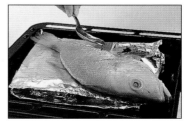

BAKING

Baking is one of the easiest ways to cook fish. The fish is placed in an oiled dish, seasoned and moistened with a little liquid – water, wine, stock or lemon juice – then covered and baked in a 180°C (350°F/Gas 4) oven. Baked fish remains moist and flavoursome, and because it needs no handling, it is ideal for stuffing. Fish can be wrapped in buttered foil with a few herbs and a little wine or water, then placed on a baking sheet to cook gently until done.

1 Prepare the stuffing as recipe directs. Fill the cavities of the fish or season the fillets or steaks. Butter an ovenproof dish and sprinkle with a small finely chopped onion or 2 shallots. Arrange the fish in the dish and brush the tops with butter or oil. Sprinkle with 3–4 tablespoons lemon juice or wine and bake covered until just cooked.

2 To bake in foil: butter or oil a long piece of foil. Lay the fish in the centre and season.

3 Sprinkle with 2–3 tablespoons wine, water or lemon juice and wrap the fish, neatly folding the foil like an envelope, allowing air space inside the foil. Set on a baking sheet and bake in a 200°C (400°F/Gas 6) oven, about 20 minutes for up to a 900g (2lb) whole fish, longer if the fish weighs more.

Almost any fish fillets can be cooked in this way. Try turbot, sea bass, snapper or even salmon.

Baking in paper, *en papillote*, is a wonderful way to bake and present fish. The paper turns a golden brown, and the delicious smell and flavour of the fish can be fully savoured when the package is opened at the table. This method is surprisingly easy for a small dinner party, since the fish can be assembled ahead, refrigerated, and then placed in a hot oven for about 20 minutes before serving.

FISH FILLETS IN PAPER

1 Cut four pieces of baking parchment at least 45cm (18in) long and fold in half lengthways. Cut the open side into a rounded half-heart shape. Open the papers to a full heart and brush each with butter or oil.

2 Arrange a quarter of each of the vegetables and bacon, if using, on the centre of a paper heart next to the fold. Arrange fish fillets on top, sprinkle with a quarter of the herbs, oil and wine. Season to taste.

INGREDIENTS

2 small carrots, julienned
2 small leeks, julienned
1 medium tomato, peeled, seeded, and chopped
2 rashers bacon, diced and cooked until crisp (optional)
4 fish fillets (about 200g/7oz each) cut in half
2 tablespoons chopped fresh herbs, such as dill, tarragon, chives or basil
4 tablespoons olive oil
4 tablespoons dry white wine or fish stock
Salt and freshly ground black pepper

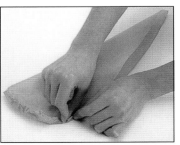

3 Fold the other side of the paper over the filling and, beginning at the rounded edge, fold and twist the edge together as if crimping pastry, to form an airtight package. Tuck the edge under. Repeat with remaining paper packages.

4 Slide packages onto a large baking sheet and bake in a 200°C (400°F/Gas 6) oven for about 10 minutes, until the paper is browned and puffed up. Slide onto individual plates and allow diners to open their own.

CRUSTACEANS

CRAB AND CRAYFISH

Crab is eaten hot or cold, out of the shell, or dressed. In some Chinese dishes, for example, crabs are often boiled or sautéed. There are many kinds of crabs, but the only one eaten shell and all is the soft-shell blue crab, a delicacy found along the east coast of the United States in season. Fresh uncooked crab should be alive when purchased and refrigerated on a tray of ice until ready to cook, preferably on the same day.

Most crayfish (also called crawfish) is harvested from fresh-water rivers and ponds. The white tail meat is used in many dishes, and the heads add richness to Cajun and Creole stocks and stews. You can buy cooked or live crayfish; peeled tails are available fresh or frozen. Live crayfish should smell fresh when purchased and be refrigerated immediately after purchase. Use within 2 days.

If crayfish are muddy, soak in cold, salted water for 15 minutes before cooking. Drain and rinse; repeat if necessary. Cook as for crab (see right), boiling for 3–5 minutes until shells turn bright red.

LOBSTER

Lobster is eaten poached, steamed, baked or grilled, and is served hot or cold. It is one of the most popular shellfish. There are two main varieties of lobster: the *American* or *Maine* lobster has claws and a tail full of meat. *Spiny* or *rock* lobsters have no claws, so all the meat is in the tail.

Whole lobster is sold live or cooked. Lobster tails are available cooked or uncooked, fresh or frozen. Choose the most active of live lobsters and check that it feels heavy for its size, with a tail that curls under well. Cooked lobster should have a bright red colour and the tail should spring back quickly when uncurled. Cook live lobsters on the same day as purchased or refrigerate on damp paper on an ice-filled pan. Freezing the lobster for 10–15 minutes before cooking will immobilize it completely. (Crab can also be immobilized by this method.)

SHRIMP AND PRAWNS

Tiny shrimp and larger prawns the most popular shellfish. The firm, sweet flesh is slightly briny and lends itself to many kinds of preparation. Served hot or cold, it is available year round, fresh or frozen.

PREPARING CRAB

Bring a large stockpot of water to the boil over high heat. Add 1 tablespoon salt for each 450g (1lb) crab or shellfish. Quickly lower crab into water, cover, and return to the boil. Reduce heat and simmer about 15 minutes. Drain and rinse under cold running water to cool.

1 Set the cooked crab on a work surface. Holding the body firmly, twist the legs and claws away from the body.

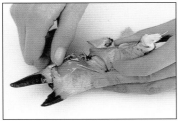

2 Use kitchen scissors to snip open the shell on the side of the leg. Pull out the meat with a skewer or crab pick.

3 Crack the claws with the back of a knife. Discard pieces of the broken shell by hand and extract the meat with a pick or skewer.

4 Lift up the "apron" (tail flap), twisting it off; discard. To open the body, hold it with one hand. Pry off the top shell with the other hand at the point where the apron was removed.

5 Discard the "dead men's fingers" (soft gills) from the sides of the body and crack the body into pieces.
6 Pick out the pieces of meat with a pick or skewer, discarding any pieces of shell or cartilage. The meat can then be eaten cold or used in salads and many other dishes.

REMOVING MEAT FROM CRAYFISH

1 Remove the tail by twisting the head away from the body, to separate the tail. Peel the two uppermost sections of shell from the tail section to expose some of the meat.

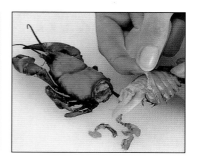

2 Turn the tail so the underside faces up. With your thumb, press the end of the tail to loosen the meat. Alternatively, snip the underside with kitchen scissors, then loosen.

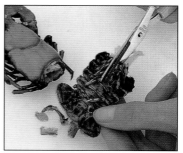

3 Gently wiggle and pull tail meat out in one piece.

4 Peel the intestinal vein from the back of the tail, starting from the body end and pulling toward the tail.

BOILING AND GRILLING LOBSTER

Prepare water as for crab (see page 91). Lower the immobilized lobster headfirst into the boiling water. Return water to boiling point and simmer for about 20 minutes, until shells are bright red. Drain and rinse under cold running water.

1 To grill: treat as above but cook for 5 minutes. Rinse and dry. Place on a large cutting board, soft underside facing up and, using kitchen scissors, cut soft shell lengthwise from head to tail. Discard all organs, the red coral (roe), and green liver (tomalley).

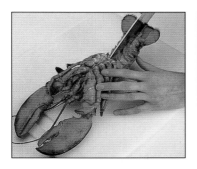

2 Snip away the sides of the soft shell. Then, using a large heavy knife, cut lengthways down the body and tail, through the thick back shell.

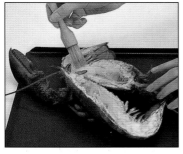

3 Press open and lay flat on a baking sheet and brush with melted butter. Broil about 10.5cm (4in) from heat for about 6 minutes, until meat is firm and opaque. Serve immediately with melted clarified butter.

REMOVING MEAT FROM LOBSTER

The cooked shell can be used to present the lobster meat. Pierce the tail to drain the excess water before cutting up the lobster.

1 Put the lobster on a cutting board, hard shell up. Holding firmly with one hand, pierce the shell between the body and tail, cutting down through the tail. Turn the lobster around and cut through the head; you will have 2 halves.

2 Remove and discard the head sac from each side (the roe and liver are edible). Remove the claws and legs by twisting off the body. Set aside.

3 Remove the intestinal vein running along the back of the shell and discard.

4 Lift the tail meat out of the shell and set aside.

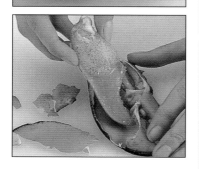

5 Crack the claws in a few places with a heavy knife or nutcracker. Remove large pieces of shell and pull out the claw meat in one piece, if possible. Repeat with remaining shell.

6 Use skewers to remove meat from the smaller legs.

COOKING PRAWNS

To boil fresh raw prawns, drop into just simmering salted water for 1–3 minutes until the shells turn pink. Rinse under cold running water. Drain and dry. Refrigerate until ready to serve. Fresh or frozen, cooked or raw, peel all prawns the same way. The heads and shells can be easily removed with your fingers. The tiny brown shrimp are often eaten whole. The shells can be used to make a shellfish soup or stock.

1 Twist and pull the head from the body.

2 Peel away the shell from the body, leaving the end of the tail for a special presentation, if you like.

3 Use a sharp knife to slit the back along the entire curve to remove the intestinal vein. Pull out the black thread with a knife or the fingers.

BUTTERFLYING PRAWNS:
To butterfly prawns for grilling, cut deeply along the back of deveined prawn without cutting all the way through. Press open to flatten. Butterflied shrimp can be battered and fried.

PRAWN COUNT

The size or "count" is important, because the number of prawns making up 450g (1lb) can vary. When calculating how many prawns are needed per person, remember that 900g (2lb) of uncooked prawns in the shell will yield about 450g (1lb) of meat after shelling and deveining.

Jumbo prawns	up to 15 per 450g (lb)		Medium prawns	approx 31–40 per 450g (per lb)
Extra large prawns	approx 16–20 per 450g (lb)		Shrimps	40+ per 450g (per lb)
Large prawns	approx 21–30 per 450g (lb)			

MOLLUSCS

Mussels and clams are bivalves which should be bought alive and very fresh.

Mussels have a smooth, shiny black shell which is sometimes covered with stone-like barnacles. The "beard", a stringy cord which ties the mussel to its pole, protrudes from the shell. Mussels are usually steamed open in a seasoned liquid, but can be eaten raw on the half shell or used in soups and salads.

There are two varieties of clam. Hard-shell clams include the small sweet littlenecks, cherrystones and the large chowder clams, minced and used in soups and sauces. Softshell clams include longneck clams – whose necks stick out from the shell – and steamers. These clams have a softer texture than hard-shell clams and are usually steamed, although they are excellent fried or chopped for chowders.

Mussels and clams should be alive when purchased; the shells should be tightly closed or close quickly when tapped sharply. Discard any that do not. Refrigerate them, covered with a damp cloth, and use within a day or two.

OYSTERS AND SCALLOPS

There are two kinds of oysters: native oysters, usually eaten raw, are differentiated by the names of the places in which they thrive. The second type, the Portuguese – despite the name – originates in the Pacific, is more elongated, and has a craggier shell than the natives. Oysters are farmed throughout Europe, the United States and Australia, are graded by size, although the grading systems are not uniform. In Britain, sizes range from 1, the largest, to 4, the smallest, and in France from 000, the largest, to 4, the smallest.

Although most often served raw on the half shell, oysters can be poached or baked, and are used in soups, stews and fish dishes. Oysters can be refrigerated on seaweed on a bed of ice for up to one week.

There are two kinds of scallops: the larger sea scallops and the tiny bay scallops. Both types are trawled or dredged at sea and are shelled and cleaned at sea because they die quickly out of water. The crescent-shaped coral is often discarded during shelling at sea, but in many places, it is much prized and is eaten with the tender, sweet white meat.

CLEANING AND OPENING MUSSELS AND CLAMS

Do not store mussels or clams in fresh water or they will die.

1 Use a stiff kitchen brush to scrub mussels and clams under cold running water. (Soak clams in sea or salted water, adding a spoonful of flour to make clams expel any sand.)

2 Using a small, sharp knife, pull off beards from shells.

3 To open: hold the hinged end against a heavy cloth in your hand. Working over a bowl, insert a sturdy, blunt knife between the shell halves, working it around to cut the hinge muscle.

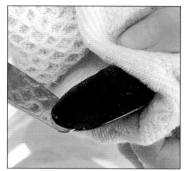

4 Twist the knife to pry open the shell. Use the tip of the knife to free the clam or mussel from the shell, allowing it to fall into the bowl with any juices. Refrigerate until ready to use.

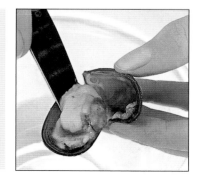

COOKING MUSSELS OR CLAMS

Steamed in a little wine with aromatics and sprinkled with parsley, mussels are deliciously sweet. Clams can be cooked in the same way, but are more often steamed open and served with melted butter, or battered and deep fried.

1 To steam: put a little dry white wine, fish stock, or water into a large stockpot with 2 tablespoons chopped parsley and any other flavourings as directed in the recipe.

2 Add the mussels or clams, cover, and bring to the boil. Cook 5–7 minutes until the shells open, shaking the pan frequently. Serve mussels or clams in their shells with their liquid.

OPENING OYSTERS

Discard any loose shell and rinse off any mud which may get into the shell, but do not wash in water or scrub.

1 Hold the oyster flat side up against one palm, covered with a thick cloth. Insert the tip of an oyster knife near the hinge, twisting to pry the shell apart.

2 Slide the knife blade along the upper shell to loosen the muscle; discard the top shell. Run the blade around the edges of the meat. Loosen the bottom. Set the half shell on ice, or tip into a bowl, if using for another dish.

SQUID

Squid, sometimes called by its Italian name, calamari, has a firm, chewy texture and agreeable flavour. It is usually cut into rings and deep-fried, or simmered in Italian or Greek-style sauces. Whole squid can be stuffed and baked. The ink is used to colour pasta and risottos. Squid is also a favourite ingredient in Japanese cooking. Fresh squid should smell sweet and fresh. Refrigerate and cook within three days. Squid is also sold frozen and prepared ready for frying. Much fresh squid is skinned and only needs the "quill" removed.

To clean squid, work over a bowl to catch the ink. Firmly grasp the head, then pull the body away from the head, tentacles and entrails. Discard entrails and reserve the ink sac, if you like. Set aside.

Pull out and discard the long, transparent quill or pen. Peel skin off the body. Rinse and pat dry.

Cut the head away from the tentacles and discard. Rinse the tentacles, dry, and cut or leave whole. Cut the body into rings for frying, chop, or leave whole for stuffing.

SPICY SQUID

INGREDIENTS

250–300g (8–10.5oz) cleaned squid
$^1/_2$ tablespoon oil
1 medium onion, sliced
170g (6 oz) fresh mushrooms,
    quartered
1 sweet green pepper, sliced
crushed red pepper flakes to taste
pinch of salt
pinch of sugar
pinch of garlic powder (optional)

1 Clean and score squid in a diagonal pattern then slice in pieces. Prepare all ingredients and put aside.

2 Heat wok to high heat with oil. Stir in the onion and the squid. Stir-fry for one minute, then add all the other ingredients. Stir until well mixed. Serve with cooked white rice.

POULTRY AND MEAT

Balancing the spread of factory-farming methods and of hormone treatments for leaner meat has been the interest in the traditional and organic rearing of farm animals. The experiences of the last few years have meant that consumers are more aware of quality and taste; all the talent and sophisticated preparation in the world cannot disguise poor ingredients.

PREPARING POULTRY AND GAME BIRDS

Domesticated birds which are reared and fattened for the table are called poultry. Chicken, turkey, duck, pigeon, guinea fowl and geese are the best known. Most poultry is sold fresh or frozen, either whole or in cut-up, ready-to-cook parts. Buy the freshest poultry possible, as it is very perishable. Poultry is highly susceptible to contamination by the *salmonella* bacteria and should be kept refrigerated.

After handling raw poultry, be sure to wash your hands, knives, cutting boards and any other equipment with which it has come in contact. Raw poultry should never come into contact with other foods, cooked or raw. Frozen poultry should be completely defrosted before cooking.

Fresh poultry should be eaten within 1–2 days after purchase. Remember the sell-by date is the final recommended day for store sale. Properly stored, it should keep for several more days. Remove any packaging, set on a plate, and cover loosely with foil or greaseproof paper. Keep refrigerated. To freeze fresh poultry, buy as fresh as possible, wrap tightly in cling film; then in freezer paper. Defrost frozen poultry overnight in the refrigerator (allow about 3–4 hours per 450g/1lb). For quick defrosting, set still completely wrapped poultry in frequently changed cold water.

PREPARING WHOLE POULTRY

Poultry should always be rinsed before use, then patted dry.

1 Remove any giblets, generally wrapped in paper or plastic, and use within a day or two. Remove any large clumps of fat around the neck and those generally tucked inside the opening of the cavity.

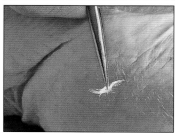

2 Remove any stray feathers on the breast. If the leg knuckles have been left on, tuck them inside the cavity, under the tip of the breastbone.

TRUSSING A WHOLE BIRD

Trussing, or tying, the bird holds it in a neat shape during cooking. Keeping a neat shape also helps ensure even cooking and, if the bird is stuffed, helps to keep in the stuffing. Trussing can be achieved with a trussing needle and string, or simply by using kitchen string to tie the bird into shape, with or without small poultry skewers. Be sure to remove any string or skewers before serving.

FOR AN UNSTUFFED BIRD:
1 Set bird, breast side up, on a board. Pull neck skin taut over the neck opening, tucking it under the backbone. Fold wing tips back and under bird to hold the neck skin.

2 Push legs down and towards the breast to plump it up. If the leg knuckles have been left on, tuck them inside the cavity, under the tip of the breastbone.

3 If leg knuckles have been cut at the first joint, bring them together, so the tip of the breastbone is resting on them, and tie together. Cut off any excess string.

FOR A STUFFED BIRD:
1 Unfold wing tips. Stuff the neck end of the bird, then pull the neck skin taut over stuffing. Use a skewer to secure it through the upper part of the backbone. Fold wing tips under the bird.

2 If you have stuffed the body cavity, close the opening with poultry skewers. Depending on the size of the bird, push as many skewers as needed through the skin on each side of the opening.

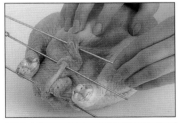

3 Using kitchen string, lace the skewers together as you would lace a boot. Tie the legs together in front of the opening as in Step 2 above.

SPATCH-COCKING POULTRY

Whole birds such as chickens, guinea fowl, pigeons and game birds are ideal for splitting and flattening. Opened up flat, they are ideal for grilling or outdoor barbecuing. Skewering the birds keeps them flat during cooking and makes for easy turning. Marinating split birds adds extra flavour and tenderness.

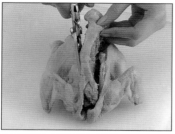

1 Cut off wing tips at the first joint. Set the bird breast side down on a cutting board. Beginning at the tail end, cut along both sides of the backbone through the skin and rib cage. Remove backbone and reserve for stock or soup.

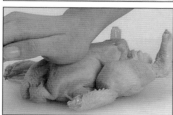

2 Turn bird breast side up and, using the heel of your hand, press down firmly on the breastbone to break it. This will flatten the bird; wipe inside the cavity with a damp kitchen paper.

3 Fold wings neatly behind the breast. Make a small slit or cut in the loose skin between the leg and lower part of the breastbone and tuck the leg end into the slit. (The bird can be skewered without this step, but skewering creates a very neat shape.)

4 Thread a long metal skewer through a wing, into the top of the breast and out through the other wing. Thread another skewer through a thigh, avoiding the bone, through the bottom tip of the breastbone, out through the other thigh.

CUTTING UP POULTRY

Although most poultry is sold in a variety of cut-up pieces, it is much more economical to buy a whole bird and portion it yourself. That way, you can cut the exact number of pieces you want and reserve the bones for stock. Most poultry and game birds have similar skeletons, so the following method should be suitable for all. To cut a bird in half, trim wing tips and cut along each side of the backbone as for spatch-cocking (page 104).

1 Using kitchen scissors, poultry shears, or a sharp knife, cut through breastbone and wishbone; the scissors or knife will naturally cut along one side, since the breastbone is pointed. You now have two halves suitable for grilling or barbecuing.

2 To cut a bird into 4 pieces, set bird breast side up on a cutting board. Using a sharp knife, cut through the loose skin between leg and breastbone; the leg will fall away from the body.

3 Cut down to the joint, then twist the leg away from the body to break the joint tendons. Cut through the ball and socket, keeping the tender "oyster", the little pad of meat tucked into the backbone.

4 Hold the top of the breast to stabilize the bird. Cut along the natural break in the rib cage to lift the breast from the lower carcass. Pull the breast and back apart and cut through the connecting joints on each side. Reserve the back for stock.

CUTTING UP POULTRY CONTINUED

5 Set the whole breast down on the cutting board. Press firmly against the breastbone to break it. Cut through breastbone and wishbone, cutting the breast in half. You now have 4 pieces.

6 Alternatively, remove the legs as in Steps 2 and 3. Steady the bird on the cutting board and cut down along the breastbone, following the rib cage, until you reach the wing joint; cut through it.

7 The previous step produces 2 boneless breast halves with the wing attached; you have a total of 4 pieces.

8 For 6 pieces, cut each breast section in half at an angle so some breast meat is included on the wing portion. (Leave a little more meat on the lower half.)

9 For 8 pieces, cut the leg portions in half at the joint, separating the thigh from the drumstick. Trim off any excess skin or fat.

BONING CHICKEN AND TURKEY BREASTS

Chicken and turkey breast joints are sold in one piece or as single breasts split along the breast bone. It is easy to remove the bones yourself.

1 To bone a whole breast, remove any excess fat and the skin, if you like. With a thin-bladed knife, cut through and along one side of the breastbone. Then, holding the knife at an angle, continue cutting down along the rib cage, removing the meat in one easy step. Repeat on the second side; you have 2 skinless, boneless breasts.

2 To remove meat from a part-boned breast quarter, cut through the wing joint to separate it from the breast; reserve the wing for stock. Remove skin from the breast. Turn the breast over and, using short strokes, scrape meat away from the bone, lifting out the bone as it becomes free.

3 Remove the long white tendon along the underside of the breast fillet as it causes the breast to curl during cooking. Loosen it at one end and pull it out with your fingers. Use the knife to help remove it. The resulting fillet is a *chicken suprême*.

4 To bone a whole turkey breast crown for stuffing, do not remove the skin. Set breast skin-side down and, starting at the far side, scrape meat away from the rib cage up to the ridge of the breastbone. Repeat on the other side.

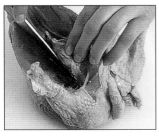

5 Use a knife to free the top of the breastbone from the meat. Lift it gently away from meat, pulling toward the neck end. Use the knife to scrape meat away from the breastbone, if necessary, being careful not to cut the skin.

PREPARING CUTLETS

Turkey breast meat makes excellent cutlets for quick cooking. Cutting across the grain provides long, attractive slices which won't shrink and curl when cooked.

1 Remove the breasts from the bone. Holding a sharp knife at a slight angle, cut long slices crosswise, about 0.5cm ($^1/_4$ in) thick.

2 Lay the slices between 2 sheets of plastic wrap. Pound with a meat mallet or bottom of a skillet to flatten to about 0.3cm ($^1/_8$ in) thick.

PREPARING BREASTS FOR STUFFING

Plump chicken or duck breasts make an elegant dish when stuffed.

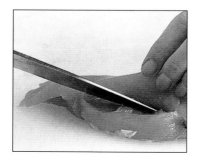

Using a boneless breast, cut horizontally into the thickest part of each breast, making a wide, deep pocket; be careful not to cut all the way through the meat. Stuff as the recipe directs.

COOKING AND CARVING POULTRY

Poultry is the world's most popular bird. Roasting, grilling, barbecuing, pan frying, sautéing and deep-frying are all dry heat methods of cooking suitable for younger, tender birds. Getting the time and temperature right is important to achieve both a crisp, golden skin and moist, tender flesh.

Poultry can be moist-heat cooked using various methods. Braising is generally used for larger, older birds. After browning, a mixture of wine, stock and vegetables is added and then simmered until tender. Stewing is ideal treatment for mature birds; the French *coq au vin* is a classic example of a chicken stew.

A sauté is a good way of cooking tender, young birds or pieces. First the pieces are browned in butter or oil; then a little liquid added, and pieces are simmered over low heat until done. After removing the pieces, the cooking juices are usually reduced or thickened.

Poaching is a good method for cooking older birds, although it also works well for small, tender pieces. The bird can be stuffed or unstuffed, but if it is stuffed, it must be carefully closed so the stuffing does not leak out or the stock seep in.

BROILING TIMES FOR POULTRY

The times given below are a guide. Begin by testing to see if it is cooked at the lowest end of the time range. Cook 10–15cm (4–6in) from the heat source; lower slightly if the meat is browning too quickly.

Roasting chicken, split in half or spatch-cocked	30–40 minutes
Guinea fowl, spatch-cocked	25–30 minutes
Pigeon, spatch-cocked	20–25 minutes
Poussin, spatch-cocked	20–25 minutes
Chicken pieces	30–35 minutes
Boneless chicken/duck breast	10–12 minutes

ROASTING POULTRY

Large birds such as capon, turkey and goose should be started at a high temperature to give crisp brown skin, then cooked through evenly at a lower temperature to maintain moisture. Do not sprinkle herbs on the outside of the bird at the beginning of cooking, as they may scorch or burn. With the exception of ducks and geese, poultry should be basted with the cooking juices during cooking to help retain moisture.

1 Rinse bird and dry well inside and out. Before trussing, loosen the breast skin with your fingers by gently easing it away from the flesh.

2 Spread softened butter mixed with herbs, garlic, or lemon zest on the flesh of the breast and stuff the cavity. Pull the neck skin over tightly and truss as directed (page 102–103). Spread a little more butter (or oil) on the breast, if desired.

TO PREPARE DUCKS AND GEESE FOR ROASTING: Truss without adding any extra fat. Prick the skin to allow the fat to drain off. Repeat the procedure twice during roasting.

TO PREPARE SMALL GAME BIRDS:
1 Small game birds should be basted or covered with bacon to prevent lean flesh from drying out.

2 Set prepared bird, breast side up, on a rack in a roasting pan. Small game birds should be started breast side down (this keeps the juices in the breast).

3 Roast bird according to the roasting chart on page 113, or as the recipe directs. Cover with foil if the bird browns too quickly. Baste occasionally after the first half hour using accumulated cooking juices every 10–15 minutes.

4 Put the bird on a carving board, cover loosely with foil, and allow to rest about 15 minutes (longer for larger birds) before carving. Use the cooking juices to make a pan gravy, if you like.

CARVING A WHOLE BIRD

Resting the bird before carving allows the juices to recede back into the flesh, resulting in plump, moist meat. Set the bird on a carving board with a well to catch the juices and remove trussing strings. Spoon any stuffing into serving dish and keep warm.

CHICKEN:
Using a long knife (or electric knife), cut through the skin between the thigh and body. Continue cutting through to the ball-and-socket joint, then twist the leg away from the body. Cut the thigh and drumstick apart.

TURKEY:
1 If carving turkey, slice the dark meat from the drumstick and arrange on a warm serving plate. Slice the darker thigh meat, or leave the thigh whole. Leave thighs and drumsticks whole when carving chicken or other smaller birds.

2 Insert a carving fork into the wing to steady the bird and carve long, 0.3–0.5-cm ($^1/_8$–$^1/_4$ in) slices at an angle, parallel to the rib cage. Cut off the wing. Carve the other side. Arrange the wings and slices on the serving plate with the dark meat.

If you decide to stuff a bird, be sure the stuffing is prepared ahead and is completely cooled to room temperature.

3 Alternatively, remove the whole breast in a single piece. Then carve the whole breast crosswise into thin slices.

ROASTING TIMES FOR POULTRY

The internal temperature of cooked poultry should reach 74–76°C (165–170°F) when an instant-read thermometer is inserted into the bird's thigh. The following times are for unstuffed birds; allow about 25–30 minutes more cooking time for stuffed birds.

BIRD AND WEIGHT	OVEN TEMPERATURE	TIME (hours)
Chicken		
1–1.3kg (2$^1/_2$–3lb)	190°C (375°F)	1–1$^1/_4$
1.5–1.8kg (3$^1/_2$–4lb)	190°C (375°F)	1$^1/_4$–1$^3/_4$
1.8–2.7kg (4–6lb)	190°C (375°F)	1$^1/_2$–2$^1/_2$
Capon		
2.2–3.1kg (5–7lb)	163°C (325°F)	1$^3/_4$–2
Turkey		
3.6–5.4kg (8–12lb)	190°C (375°F)	3–4
5.4–7.2kg (12–16lb)	163°C (325°F)	4–5
7.2–9 kg (16–20lb)	163°C (325°F)	4$^1/_2$–5
over 9kg (20lb)	163°C (325°F)	5–6
Turkey breast (whole)		
1.8–2.7kg (4–6lb)	163°C (325°F)	1$^1/_2$–2$^1/_4$
2.7–5.4kg (6–8lb)	163°C (325°F)	2$^1/_4$–3$^1/_2$
Turkey drumsticks		
450–750g (1–1$^1/_2$lb)	163°C (325°F)	1$^1/_4$–1$^3/_4$
Whole duckling		
1.5kg (3$^1/_2$lb)	190°C (375°F)	1$^3/_4$–2$^1/_2$
Goose		
3.5–4.5kg (8–10lb)	176°C (350°F)	2$^1/_2$–3
4.5–7kg (10–12lb)	176°C (350°F)	3–3$^1/_2$
Pigeon		
350–400g (12–14oz)	188°C (370°F)	40–50 min.

GRILLING AND BARBECUING

Grilling and barbecuing are popular methods of cooking all types of poultry. Spatch-cocked small birds or cut-up pieces are ideal. Marinating beforehand helps flavour the meat as well as tenderize it, but is not essential.

1 Put spatch-cocked birds or pieces in a glass or stainless steel pan and add the marinade. Leave in for at least 1 hour or overnight. Prepare an outdoor grill or preheat the grill. Line a grill pan with foil and arrange the drained birds or poultry pieces on the pan, or on an oiled rack over the fire.

2 Broil or barbecue about 10–15cm (4–6in) from the heat, about 20 minutes for a spatch-cocked bird or 10 minutes for poultry pieces, turning once and basting with the marinade halfway through cooking. (If not using a marinade, brush the poultry with a little oil and season with salt and pepper.)

STIR-FRY

Poultry is a popular choice for stir-frying. Use tender pieces cut into small even sizes, so they cook evenly.

1 Heat a wok or large skillet over high heat. Add 1–2 tablespoons oil and swirl to coat the bottom and side of the wok. Add any flavourings as directed (garlic, ginger, spring onions); stir-fry 30 seconds.

2 Add cut-up poultry pieces and any marinade; cook, stir-frying until lightly coloured, 1–2 minutes.

3 Add any other ingredients and continue as recipe directs.

FRYING CHICKEN

Fried chicken with its crisp brown coating and tender, juicy meat is a flavoursome way of preparing chicken. Dry the chicken well, since any moisture will cause the oil to spatter. Chicken pieces can be battered or coated with crumbs.

1 Heat a mixture of oil and butter in a large, heavy-basd frying pan over medium-high heat. Add the pieces, skin side down, working in batches, if necessary.

2 Fry, turning to brown well on all sides, until cooked through. This will take at least 25 minutes. Remove the breast pieces before the thighs and drumsticks, since they cook more quickly. Drain on kitchen paper.

TO DEEP-FRY:
1 Flour the pieces lightly, then dip into a mixture of beaten egg and milk. Coat lightly with seasoned flour, cornmeal or crumbs. Refrigerate 20 minutes to set the coating. If battering, dip the pieces into the batter and immediately lower into the hot oil.

2 Fill a deep-fat fryer or deep saucepan or casserole with 7.5–10cm (3–4in) oil. Heat over medium-high heat to 185°C (365°F); a small cube of bread tossed into the oil will brown in just under a minute. Using tongs or a fish slice, carefully lower the pieces into the oil; do not overcrowd or the temperature of the oil will drop. Fry until deep golden and cooked through, turning to colour evenly, 25–30 minutes.

3 Drain on paper towels. Keep warm in a low oven while frying any remaining pieces.

POT ROASTING

Pot roasting is a general term for cooking in a covered casserole. The whole bird is generally browned first, then cooked in its own juices or in a little stock, together with root vegetables like onions, potatoes and carrots. The bird can be stuffed or unstuffed, but if stuffed, be sure it is well sealed to avoid any leakage.

1 Heat 2–3 tablespoons vegetable oil in a heavy-bottom casserole just big enough to hold the bird and any vegetables. Brown the bird, turning on all sides.

2 Add about 225ml (8 fl oz) stock and any flavourings – such as a bay leaf and a few fresh thyme sprigs – and any vegetables. Bring to the boil over medium-high heat, cover, and transfer to a preheated 180°C (350°F) oven.

3 Cook for about 1^1/$_4$ hours, or until the bird is cooked through. The juices will run clear, and the legs will move freely in their sockets when wiggled.

Carefully place the bird on a cutting board. Remove the strings and discard. Spoon the stuffing into a dish. Meanwhile, reduce the juices over high heat, scraping up any bits on the bottom of the pan. Strain the gravy over the bird or serve separately.

GAME BIRDS: Care must be taken not to let the meat dry out. For roasting, birds should be barded or covered with bacon.

CHOOSING AND PREPARING MEAT

In general, look for well-cut, well-trimmed meat; smaller cuts, such as steaks and chops, should be evenly cut or sliced so they cook at the same rate. Flesh colour should be clear but not bright, with no grey or yellow tinges and no dry edges. Beef should be well marbled – that is, lightly streaked with flecks of fat. Exterior fat should be creamy white, feel firm and have a soft, waxy texture. All meat should smell fresh and look moist. Yellow fat can indicate old meat.

Select the cut most appropriate to the cooking method you are using. Tender cuts from the loin, fillet and saddle (the back of the animal) are most suitable for dry-heat cooking methods such as roasting, grilling or frying. Less tender cuts from the top of the rump, flank or breast are more suitable for pot-roasting or braising, both moist-heat cooking methods.

As a general rule, allow about 170–198g (6–7oz) of boneless lean meat per person. For meat on the bone such as a rib roast, allow about 227–340g (8–12oz) per person, and for very bony meats such as spare ribs, 450g (1lb) per person is needed. The preceding is very much a personal choice.

Store meat on a plate in the coldest part of the refrigerator. The temperature should be 2–4.5°C (30–35°F). Loosely cover pre-cut meats; wrapping tightly encourages the development of bacteria. Store prepackaged meat in its container. Never allow any meat to come into contact with other foods, raw or cooked. Larger cuts will keep longer than smaller cuts and pieces: beef and lamb will keep slightly longer than pork or veal. Minced meat should be cooked within 2 days if prepacked, one day if bought loose. Frozen meat should be thawed overnight in a refrigerator, not at room temperature or even under cold running water.

All meats harbour bacteria. Bacteria increase rapidly at room temperature and can cause meat to spoil. Refrigeration slows down the process and freezing stops it, although bacteria will begin to multiply when the meat is thawed. Cooking at high temperatures kills the bacteria, but they can still be present in lightly cooked meat. Pregnant women, children, the elderly and people with serious health conditions should avoid raw or lightly cooked meats.

Always wash your hands, knives, cutting boards and any other utensils used to prepare raw or cooked meats. Ideally, meat should be cooked thoroughly to kill all bacteria. Once cooked, cool leftover meat as quickly as possible, then refrigerate.

PREPARING MEATS

Even meats prepared by the butcher or bought ready-to-eat in the supermarket may need extra trimming before cooking. As a general rule, remove as much exterior fat as possible. Use a sharp knife to remove any rind or skin and thick fat from the surface of the meat. A thin layer (about 0.3cm/ $^1/_8$ in) can be left on large roasting pieces. Leave a little fat on steaks or chops for grilling, but slash the edges or snip with kitchen scissors at 1.5-cm ($^1/_2$-in) intervals to prevent curling during cooking. When trimming meats, trim the fat and any gristle from bones and wrap with foil to prevent burning. Cut out any sinews or tough connective tissues, sliding the point of a sharp knife underneath to loosen it, then cut away.

TO CHINE A LARGE CUT:
Remove or loosen the backbone where it is joined to the ribs. Any cut such as rib roasts, loin roasts and even small racks of lamb should be chined with a meat saw; it is best to ask your butcher to do this. Supermarket cuts are usually prepared in this way, to allow for easier carving. If you like, remove the backbone completely.

TO BARD A ROAST:
The technique of barding is usually done to protect a large cut which is to be roasted. Cover the meat (or game) with thin slices of beef or pork fat, or bacon, and tie in place with string. As the meat cooks, the fat or bacon slowly melts and bastes the meat, keeping it moist. Remove and discard the fat before serving; the crisp bacon can be served alongside the meat if you like.

AVOID using wooden cutting boards which are difficult to clean or disinfect. White, non-porous chopping boards can be scrubbed with hot water and disinfected or put into the dishwasher.

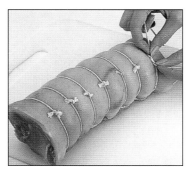

TO TIE A BONED PIECE OF MEAT:
Large cuts which can be bought boned for stuffing or easier carving need to be tied into a firm, neat shape before cooking. After stuffing or seasoning, reshape the meat into a neat roll. Use string to tie the meat at 2.5-cm (1-in) intervals before roasting or pot-roasting.

TENDERIZING MEATS

Meat can be tenderized by pounding, scoring or marinating. These techniques break down the fibres in the meat, rendering them more tender and adding flavour.

VEAL SCALLOPS OR THIN STEAKS:
1 To pound thin cuts such as veal scallops or thin steaks, lay the meat between 2 sheets of cling film or greaseproof paper; pound with a meat mallet, rolling pin or bottom of a heavy-based pan.

2 Use a sharp knife to score the meat lightly in a diamond pattern. This technique literally cuts through many of the tougher fibres.

Marinades can be cooked or "raw", but usually contain a mixture of oil; an acid such as vinegar, lemon or lime juice; and herbs and flavourings. The acid acts to tenderize the meat; the oil acts as a lubricant, and, of course, the herb adds flavour. Allow cooked marinades to cool completely before adding to the meat.

CUTTING THE FILLET: BEEF

FOR ROASTING WHOLE:
Fold the tapered end under to make an even shape or cut off 10–12.5cm (4–5 in) from the tapered end to make an even shape; use the trimmed ends for kebabs or stroganoff. If you like, bard and then tie the fillet.

TO CUT INTO STEAKS:
Trim off the end as above. Beginning from the thick (neck) end, cut about four 4-cm (1¹/₂-in) thick slices; these are called *Tournedos* or *Filet Mignon*. Cut the centre section into two 12.5-cm (5-in) pieces of *Chateaubriand* (these are roasted at high heat); cut the remaining meat into 2.5-cm (1-in) fillet steaks.

1 Cut and trim away as much fat as possible, then cut away the "chain muscle", which lies to the side of the main meat. Use it for stewing or mincing.

2 Pull out the "silverskin" or tight tissue coating which surrounds the meat. Slide the point of a knife under it and scrape away from the meat, leaving the meat completely clean beneath.

CUTTING MEAT FOR STEWS

To cut cubes of meat for stewing, start with a large piece of chuck or braising steak. Trim away as much fat and gristle as possible. Cut the meat into 5-cm (2-in) cubes.

BONING A LOIN OF LAMB FOR ROASTING

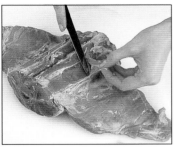

1 To bone a lamb loin or saddle (double loin) for roasting, set the trimmed loin skin side up on a work surface and trim the "fell" (the papery layer of connective tissue) from the surface. Trim the surface fat to about 0.5 cm ($^1/_4$ in).

2 Turn the saddle or loin over and trim as much fat from the underside as possible.

3 Starting from the centre of the backbone, slide the knife between the tenderloin and the rib bones. Cut the flesh away from the bone, but leave the meat attached to the flank. Continue until all the rib bones on one side have been freed. Repeat on the other side.

4 Slide the knife under the back and rib bones, separating the meat from the ribs and backbone.

5 Using your hands, pull out the backbone from the meat, leaving the loins intact.

6 Roll the flank flaps towards the centre from each side. Tie the roast with kitchen string at 2.5-cm (1-in) intervals. The meat is ready for roasting.

CUTTING VEAL ESCALOPES

Veal escalopes are the most popular veal cut. The best escalopes come from the fillet end of the leg, but they can also be cut from the best end of neck or shoulder.

1 Cut all fat and sinews from a piece of leg fillet at least 12.5cm (5 in) wide. Holding a long, sharp knife diagonally at an angle, cut across the meat into slices about 0.3–0.6cm ($1/8$–$1/4$in) thick.

2 Lay the slices between 2 sheets of cling film. Pound to flatten and tenderize, being careful not to make holes or tear the meat.

CUTTING NOISETTES FROM A LOIN

1 To cut lamb or pork noisettes from a loin, remove the loin meat by cutting down along the backbone and along the ribs. Pull out the bone. Trim the tenderloin evenly, leaving a thin layer of fat. Roll up the loin and tie at intervals with string.

2 Using the string as a guide to size, cut the tenderloin into small noisettes 1.9–2.5cm ($3/4$–1in) thick.

BONING, ROLLING AND BUTTERFLYING A LAMB LEG

Partially boning a leg of lamb makes for much easier carving. Boning it completely leaves it free for stuffing and rolling, or for butterflying – opening up flat for grilling, roasting or barbecuing. Trim off the fell and as much exterior fat as possible. To remove the pelvic bone – made up of the aitchbone and hipbone – set the leg on a cutting board with the pelvic bone facing up.

1 With a sharp boning knife, cut around the exposed ball and socket joint between the hipbone and main leg bone. Free it from the meat. Cut completely around the pelvic bone and remove it.

2 Beginning at the top of the exposed leg bone, cut down along the bone through the meat, from the top to the knee joint. Using short, quick strokes, curl and scrape the meat from the bone all the way around.

3 Continue cutting along the length of the shank bone, cutting and scraping the meat away; the bone should be almost free. Lift out the leg bone and cut around the knee joint, freeing the meat completely. Remove as many tendons as possible by scraping them away from the meat.

TO ROLL THE MEAT FOR ROASTING:
Season, and if you like, spread the stuffing along the centre. Roll as neatly as possible, tucking in the small end piece. Tie at 2.5-cm (1-in) intervals. The boned leg is ready for roasting.

TO BUTTERFLY THE LEG:
Lay the meat flat on the work surface, boned side up. Holding the knife parallel to the meat, slit open the thick upper portion to create a slab of even thickness. Trim any remaining fat or tendons.
To keep the meat flat during cooking, thread 2 or 3 long metal skewers through at the widest part. This also makes the meat easier to turn.

DRY-HEAT COOKING METHODS

There are two general types of cooking methods: dry heat and moist heat. Dry heat methods include roasting, grilling, baking, sautéing pan and deep-frying. Foods cooked by dry-heat methods have a richer flavour caused by browning, which caramelizes the natural sugars in the meats or other foods. Cooking by dry heat involves applying heat directly or indirectly.

ROASTING MEAT:
ROAST PRIME RIB OF BEEF WITH PAN GRAVY

The fierce dry heat of oven roasting is perfect for tender cuts of most meats. Leaner meats can be barded or marinated. Bring meat to room temperature before roasting so that it cooks evenly. Cook smaller roasts like lamb racks or beef tenderloin at high temperatures for good surface colour; large cuts cook better and shrink less if cooked at a lower constant temperature.

INGREDIENTS

3-rib prime rib roast, backbone chined, about 4.5kg (10lb)
salt and freshly ground pepper
1 large onion, quartered
2 carrots, cut into 5-cm (2-in) pieces
1 stalk celery, cut into 5-cm (2-in) pieces
350ml (12 fl oz) beef stock

1 Preheat oven to 180°C (350°F/Gas 4). Brush a roasting pan with oil, then rub the surface of the meat with remaining oil. Season meat with salt and pepper.

2 Put cut-up vegetables in the roasting pan. Set the meat on top, fat side up. Roast beef for 20 minutes per 450g (1lb) until a meat thermometer inserted in the thickest part of the meat reads 54.5°C (135°F) for medium-rare beef.

3 Transfer beef to a carving board and cover with a foil tent. Allow to rest for 15–20 minutes.

MAKING PAN GRAVY

1 To make pan gravy, spoon off all but 1–2 tablespoons of fat from the pan drippings. Set the pan over medium-high heat and, when the juices begin to boil, sprinkle in the flour. Using a wooden spoon, scrape up the browned bits on the bottom of the pan until a smooth paste or "roux" forms.

2 Gradually pour in stock, stirring constantly until a smooth gravy is formed. Allow to come to a boil, then season with salt and pepper, and simmer about 5 minutes. Strain the gravy into a gravy boat and keep warm.

TESTING TO SEE IF IT IS COOKED

Large roasts will continue cooking for up to ten minutes after being removed from the heat.

USING A MEAT THERMOMETER:

To use a meat thermometer, insert it through the fat side of the meat, being careful not to touch bone. Bone conducts heat faster, and you'll get a false reading of the meat's temperature. To be an accurate indicator, a meat thermometer must be inserted properly.

For red meat, roasts, steaks or chops: Insert the thermometer in the centre of the thickest part, away from bone, fat and gristle.
For poultry: Insert it in the inner thigh area near the breast of the bird, but not touching bone.
For minced meat and poultry: Place it in the thickest area; insert sideways in thin items such as pasties.

CARVING A RIB ROAST

All roasted meats should rest in a warm place before carving; tenting with foil helps to keep the meat warm. Resting allows meat to relax and reabsorb juices which would otherwise be lost when the meat is carved. A large cutting board with a well to collect the juices is ideal. Meat cuts vary, but most should be cut across the grain; the more tender the meat, the thicker the slices can be.

1 Holding the meat with a carving fork, slice horizontally along the rib bones to remove them completely.

2 Place the meat boned side down and slice crosswise into thick or thin slices. Alternatively, slice downward between the ribs, leaving a rib on each alternate slice.

MEAT ROASTING TIMETABLE

The following times are for meats started at 230°C (450°F/Gas 8) for 15 minutes, then finished at 180°C (350°F/Gas 5°). Larger cuts are better roasted at a lower constant heat.

MEAT	AMOUNT OF COOKING	THERMOMETER READING	MINS PER LB (450 G)
Beef	Rare	49.5–52°C (125–130°F)	12–15
	Medium	54.5–57°C (135–140°F)	15–18
	Well Done	59.5–62°C (145–160°F)	18–20
Veal	Well Done	62°C (160°F)	18–20
Lamb	Rare	52–54.5°C (130–135°F)	15
	Medium	57–59.5°C (140–145°F)	15–18
	Well Done	62°C (160°F)	18–20
Pork	Well Done	62–67°C (160–165°F)	20–25

CARVING A RACK OF LAMB

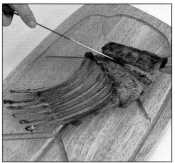

1 Set the meat on a cutting board with the backbone on your left. Remove the chined bone.

2 Holding the rack with the ribs in the air, carve downwards with the knife, cutting cleanly between each rib.

CARVING A LEG OF LAMB

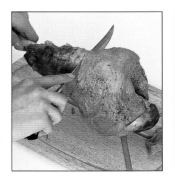

1 Set the meat on the cutting board with the shank bone on your left side. Cut off a few slices from the thin side, then set the leg on the flat surface to balance it.

2 Starting at the shank end, slice down to the leg bone until you reach the other end. Holding the knife parallel to the leg bone, cut under the slices to release them.

PAN−GRILLING AND SAUTÉING

Pan-grilling and sautéing are dry-heat methods using small amounts of fat in an open pan. As with other dry-heat methods, use tender cuts such as steaks, escalopes, slices of liver and hamburgers. Use a heavy-based pan and oil or clarified butter, since ordinary butter can burn. Sautéing uses slightly less vigorous heat and only a small amount of oil. After cooking, the juices in the pan can be deglazed to make a simple sauce.

1 Heat 2 tablespoons of oil or half oil and half butter in a heavy-based frying pan, large enough to hold the meat without crowding, over medium-high heat. Season the meat and add to the pan.

2 Fry until well browned on one side, then turn to brown on the other. For pork chops or other meats which require complete cooking, lower the heat after the initial browning to allow the meat to cook through without burning.

3 Cooking time depends on the meat, thickness of the cut and the temperature. Pressing the meat with your fingers can give an indication of how well it is cooked; the more well-done the meat, the more resistance it will offer.

TO DEGLAZE PAN JUICES

During pan-frying the meat exudes flavourful juices, and brown crusty bits form on the bottom of the pan. Adding wine, alcohol, vinegar, cream, stock or water to dissolve the sediments is called *deglazing*. This is a quick, easy way to make a simple sauce, add more flavour to stews and make gravies for roasted meats.

1 Remove cooked meat from the pan and keep warm. Tilt the pan and, using a spoon, scoop off as much fat as possible; this is called *degreasing*. Add any ingredients called for in the recipe, such as garlic, shallots, onions or mushrooms, and stir.

2 Return pan to the heat and pour in the liquid as directed by the recipe. Bring to the boil, stirring and scraping up all the sediment from the bottom of the pan.

3 Boil for 1–2 minutes or until the liquid is thickened or syrupy. Add any remaining ingredients, if the recipe indicates, and season. Serve over the pan-fried or sautéed meat.

MAKING MEAT SAUTÉS

Not to be confused with pan-grillling and sautéing meats, a meat sauté is a dish browned in oil or butter, then covered to cook gently in its own juices. Pork and veal cutlets, veal escalopes and pork tenderloin, as well as other stewing cuts of veal and lamb, are juicy cuts suitable for sautés. The meat must be cut in even-size pieces which can then be seasoned and dusted with flour before browning. Add a little deglazing liquid at the end of cooking, but the meat should never be covered with liquid.

1 Trim the fat and connective tissue from a pork tenderloin or other meat. Holding the knife at an angle, cut the tenderloin into 4 or 6 equal-size escalopes. Season with salt and pepper and dust with flour.

2 Heat 2–3 tablespoons vegetable oil, or half oil and butter, or clarified butter, in a deep, heavy-based frying pan over medium heat. Add the pieces of meat (do not crowd them) and brown gently, turning to colour evenly. *The pan should be covered during sautéing.*

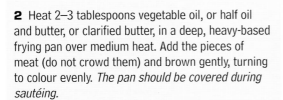

3 Drain any excess fat and, if the recipe directs, add vegetables such as baby onions, mushrooms, tomatoes or courgettes. Cover the pan and simmer until the vegetables are tender, shaking the pan frequently or turning the vegetables to brown evenly.

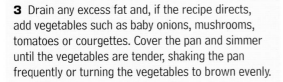

4 When the meat is fork tender, add about 125ml (4 fl oz) liquid such as wine, stock or cream to deglaze the pan (page 129) or as recipe directs. Season before serving.

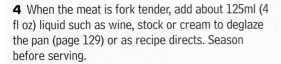

130

GRILLING MEATS

Grilling exposes food directly to the heat (flame or element), so only the best quality, tender, well-marbled cuts of meat should be used. A little exterior fat is necessary to keep the meat moist, but too much may cause the grill to flame up and burn the meat. Trim as much connective tissue as possible, since it will cause the meat to toughen. If broiling veal or pork, cook at a slightly lower temperature or a little further away from the heat source to allow the interior to cook completely while the outside browns. Marinating and basting also help keep leaner meats moist. Do not season meats until just before cooking since the salt can draw out the juices. Preheat the grill or prepare an outdoor barbecue. Line the grill rack with foil for easier cleaning. Trim as much fat as possible from the meat and remove any visible connective tissue. If the meat has been marinating, drain off excess liquid.

1 Arrange the meat on the lined rack, brush with a little oil, and season with salt and pepper.

2 The broiler rack should be about 7.5–10cm (3–4in) from the heat; if barbecuing, keep the rack about 10–15cm (4–6in)) from the heat. Cook 3–4 minutes until well-browned, then using tongs, turn the meat and cook to the desired degree of doneness. Serve with flavoured butter.

FOR THICK CUTS:
For Chateaubriand or butterflied leg of lamb, lower the grill heat or move the barbecue grill to a higher position over the coals to finish cooking, once the exterior is browned. Alternatively, after browning, transfer the meat to a preheated oven to complete cooking evenly.

STIR-FRYING

Stir-frying is based on Chinese wok cooking. The wok is a large, rounded pan which allows foods to be stirred and tossed for quick, even cooking. A special shovel-like spatula, wooden spoon or chopsticks are used for stirring. All ingredients must be prepared ahead of time. Meat and vegetables should be cut into small cubes or strips of equal size, and any aromatics or sauce ingredients prepared.

1 Slice the meat into thin strips or small cubes. Marinate briefly in a Chinese-style marinade, if desired.

2 Heat the dry wok or frying pan over medium-high heat until very hot. Pour in the oil and swirl to coat the wok completely.

3 When the oil is very hot but not smoking, add the recipe ingredients in batches, as directed. Do not overcrowd or the food will steam, rather than fry. You may need to remove one ingredient and set aside while cooking another.

4 When all the ingredients are cooked, pour in the sauce or liquid as the recipe directs. It will bubble and begin to thicken. Return any ingredients removed earlier and stir until well-coated; serve.

Moist-heat Methods

Moist-heat cooking uses moisture as well as heat to cook meat. Slow simmering for a long period tenderizes tougher cuts of meat and brings out rich flavours. The cooking liquid is then generally used to make a sauce or gravy, such as with a pot roast or silverside. However, if the meats are salted or cured, like ham or corned beef, the liquid should not be salted or used for sauce. Cooking in liquid often helps to draw some of the saltiness out of the meat. Meats subjected to moist heat are cooked to well done. Test by piercing with a fork; it should pull apart easily – hence the expression *fork-tender*. Undercooked, the meat will be tough and chewy; overcooked, the meat will fall apart or have a stringy texture.

BRAISING

Braised meats are first browned, then cooked in a liquid, which will form the base of a sauce. The long, slow-moist cooking helps tenderize the meat. This method is often used with pork roasts.

1 Over medium-high heat, heat the oil in a large, heavy flameproof casserole with a tight-fitting lid. Add the meat and brown well on all sides, turning as necessary. Remove to a plate. Add any onions or other vegetables to the casserole, stirring to colour. Pour in any other liquids, such as tomato sauce or wine, and any herbs or seasonings. Stir well to combine.

2 Return the meat to the casserole, cover tightly, and bring to the boil. Reduce heat to low and simmer $1^{1}/_{2}$–2 hours, depending on the size of the meat. Alternatively, transfer the casserole to a preheated 160°C (325°F/Gas 3) oven for $1^{1}/_{2}$–2 hours, basting occasionally. Place the meat on a cutting board, strain and degrease the sauce, season, and thicken. Slice the meat cross-ways into the slices and serve with the gravy.

133

STEWING: BEEF STEW IN RED WINE

The procedure for stewing is very similar to braising, although stews are usually made with bite-size or small pieces of meat. Stews can be brown or white. Brown stews involve browning the meat pieces before cooking in liquid. White stews include *fricassees*, which lightly sears the meat in fat without actually browning, before adding liquid, and *blanquettes*, which blanch the meat before cooking in liquid. Both dishes are white or creamy in colour.

Stews use many of the same cuts as braises, which should be well-trimmed. Using a good full-bodied stock is the key to a rich flavourful stew. Red meats such as beef, lamb or game are generally used for brown stews, while pale meats like veal, pork and chicken appear in fricassees and blanquettes. From the famous *Boeuf Bourguinon* to Moroccan *togines*, almost every cuisine has a classic stew recipe.

INGREDIENTS

115g (4oz) thick-cut bacon or lean salt
    pork, diced
1.5kg (3^1/$_2$lb) lean stewing beef,
    preferably chuck, cut into 5-cm
    (2-in) pieces
1 onion, chopped
1 carrot, chopped
3 tablespoons all-purpose flour
750ml (1^1/$_4$ pints) full-bodied dry red
    wine
2 tablespoons tomato purée
large bouquet garni (page 10)
750ml (1^1/$_4$ pints) rich beef stock
salt and pepper
2 tablespoons butter
350g (12oz) pearl onions
350g (12oz) button mushrooms,
    halved if large
2 tablespoons chopped fresh parsley

1 Put the bacon or salt pork in a large, heavy-based flameproof casserole and set over medium-high heat. As the bacon or salt pork begins to sizzle, stir occasionally. Cook until crisp and golden, then use a slotted spoon to place on a plate. Spoon off all but 2 tablespoons of the fat.

2 Add enough meat to fit in one layer and brown on all sides until well coloured; you will need to work in batches. Transfer each batch to a plate until all the meat is well browned. Pour off all but 2 tablespoons of the remaining fat.

3 Add the chopped onion, and carrot. Cook 3–4 minutes, until softened and browned, stirring frequently. Sprinkle the flour over and stir constantly.

4 Gradually pour in the wine, tomato purée and stock; season with salt and pepper. Add the bouquet garni and tie to the casserole handle. Bring vegetables and stock to the boil, scraping up the brown bits from the bottom of the pan.

5 Return meat to the casserole. Add a little more stock, if necessary, to cover the ingredients. Cover tightly and simmer gently over low heat for about 3 hours until the meat is tender.

6 About $1/2$ hour before the end of the cooking time, heat the butter in a skillet over medium-high heat. Add the pearl onions and fry, stirring frequently until golden. Remove to a plate. Add the mushrooms to the pan and sauté until golden, 3–4 minutes, stirring frequently. Add the reserved onions and the mushrooms to the stew, pushing them into the gravy.

7 Cook until the meat and vegetables are tender. Remove and discard the bouquet garni, stir in the parsley, and serve.

VEGETABLES

Though the vegetarian path is still the choice of a minority, its influence has permeated far beyond. No longer are vegetables boiled to a pulp, their vitamins lost to the water. Now the guideline is: the less cooked, the better – raw is often best. Techniques like stir-frying, steaming and roasting keep in both flavour and goodness; careful preparation too is invaluable in preserving vegetable virtues.

ROOTS AND TUBERS

Roots and tubers belong to the class of foods that basically provides energy in the human diet in the form of carbohydrates. The terms refer to any growing plant that stores edible material in a subterranean root, corm or tuber. At one time tubers were long neglected by cooks, but in recent years there has been increased attention on them because of their healthful properties.

Roots and tubers grow underground and include potatoes, sweet potatoes and yams, carrots, turnips, parsnips, celeriac (celery root), beetroot, Jerusalem artichokes, rutabaga, kohlrabi (technically a cabbage), and salsify. Red and white radishes, long radishes and daikon are also root vegetables.

Most root vegetables store well in a cool, dark place, and many can be interchanged. Most need to be cooked until just tender, and the general rule is to start cooking in cold water, bring to the boil and simmer until tender to avoid breaking up. Roots and tubers are extremely versatile and can be cooked in many ways: steamed, boiled and mashed, roasted, sautéed, baked, fried, or gratinéed. Their high water content makes them ideal for microwaving. Most roots and tubers need to be peeled before cooking, although young potatoes and carrots can be trimmed and scrubbed.

PEELERS

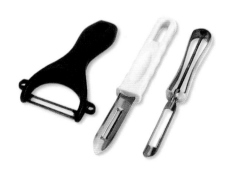

There are different kinds of peelers available. Choose a style you feel comfortable with or which is suitable to the size and shape of the vegetable, such as a wide blade for larger vegetables like potatoes, or a fixed or swivel blade for carrots or parsnips. A sharp knife is best for thicker-skinned celeriacs.

CARROTS AND PARSNIPS

Probably the sweetest of the root vegetables, carrots and parsnips are prepared in the same way. Although they can be eaten raw, parsnips are generally cooked.

PREPARING:
To prepare carrots or parsnips, trim the ends, then peel. If preparing parsnips ahead, drop into acidulated water to prevent darkening. Carrots and parsnips can be sliced into rounds, cut lengthways for roasting, cut into julienne strips for stir-frying or salads, or chopped.

COOKING:
To cook, drop into boiling salted water and simmer until tender, about 5–6 minutes for sliced carrots or parsnips; 7–9 minutes for whole baby carrots, or, cook 450g (1lb) carrots, sliced, in a deep skillet with 50ml (2 fl oz) water or stock, 15g ($^1/_2$oz) butter, and 1 tablespoon sugar or honey, tightly covered, until just tender, about 5 minutes. Uncover and allow excess liquid to evaporate until carrots are lightly glazed and tender.

BLANCHING:
To blanch parsnips for pan-frying or roasting, cover with cold water, bring to the boil, and simmer 1 minute; drain. Fry in butter until tender and golden, 8–10 minutes. To purée or mash, cook until very tender, then mash or purée.

ROASTING:
To roast parsnips, heat about 50ml (2 fl oz) oil and 1 tablespoon butter in a roasting pan. Add the blanched, drained parsnips and roast until crisp and tender, 35–40 minutes in a preheated oven at 200°C (400°F/Gas 6), turning occasionally.

POTATOES

This vegetable can be cooked in so many ways it is not possible to count them.

PREPARING:
To prepare, scrub the skins if baking. To prevent the thin skin on new potatoes from splitting, peel a strip of skin from around the centre. Otherwise, peel potatoes with a vegetable peeler. Slice, cube, dice or prepare as recipe directs.

BAKING:
To bake white or sweet potatoes, pierce each potato with a skewer or knife point in several places to prevent the potato from bursting. Arrange on a foil-lined baking sheet or directly on the oven shelf and bake in a 200°C (400°F/Gas 6) oven until tender, about 1$\frac{1}{4}$ hours.

SAUTÉEING:
To sauté or fry, heat enough oil to cover the bottom of a heavy-based frying pan over medium heat until very hot. Add the potatoes (raw or pre-cooked) and allow them to brown on one side before turning. Continue to cook until crisp and golden and tender, about 10–12 minutes.

1 To deep-fry French fries, cut peeled potatoes into sticks about 0.5cm ($\frac{1}{4}$ in) thick. Soak in cold water for $\frac{1}{2}$ hour, drain well, and dry on a clean towel.

2 Heat the oil and fry the potatoes in small batches until just tender and lightly golden, 4–6 minutes depending on their size. Remove with slotted spoon and drain on paper towels.

3 When all the potatoes have been cooked, fry them a second time at a slightly higher temperature until crisp and brown, about 2 minutes. Drain on kitchen paper, sprinkle with salt, and serve hot.

PODS, SEEDS AND CORN

This group of vegetables are the seeds of the plants; sometimes only the seed is eaten (like peas), other times, the whole pod is eaten (mange-touts). Although corn is technically a grain, the kernels we eat are actually the plant seeds. These vegetables are generally high in protein and carbohydrates.

Beans and peas are members of the legume family, vegetables with double-seamed pods containing a single row of seeds; this group contains a huge variety of green beans from around the world. In spite of regional differences, most of them are prepared and cooked in similar ways. Young varieties of edible pods, like mange-touts, are eaten in the pod while the seed is immature; shelled peas and beans, like garden peas and fresh broad beans, are removed from the pod to eat fresh. Others are left to dry (see Grains and Legumes, page 160).

Green vegetables, unlike root vegetables, are best cooked quickly by dropping into boiling salted water and boiling rapidly for 2–10 minutes until just tender, but still crisp and crunchy with a bright colour.

FRESH BEANS

Used for their edible pods, this group of immature beans includes green beans, string beans, snap beans, yellow wax beans and Chinese long beans. Trim the ends, pulling off any strings by "snapping" the stem ends and pulling the strings, which may still be attached along the sides (although many new varieties are stringless). For young, tender beans, trim with kitchen scissors or a knife. Edible pea pods such as mange-touts and the deliciously sweet sugar-snap peas are prepared the same way. All fresh beans can be eaten raw, lightly blanched, steamed, sautéed, stir-fried, or microwaved – they are best lightly cooked.

To prepare snap beans or flat beans, cut diagonally into 2.5-cm (1-in) pieces.

Long beans or flat beans are sometimes cut vertically into long slivers; beans cut this way will cook more quickly.

OKRA

Okra is an unusual, five-sided, elongated pod. Brought to the New World by African slaves and French settlers, it is now used in Creole, Cajun, Southern and Caribbean cooking. When okra is cooked for long periods of time, it develops a gelatinous texture used to thicken gumbos and stews. Choose small to medium pods with no soft spots. Okra can be boiled, stewed, pickled or deep-fried.

To prepare okra, do not wash until ready to cook. Using a small sharp knife, trim the stem evenly; avoid piercing it. Cook in stainless steel or other non-corrosive cookware to avoid discoloration.

CORN

Although corn is a grain, its kernels, like peas, are seeds. Like peas, corn contains sugars which begin turning to starch as soon as it is picked, so the fresher the corn, the better and sweeter. Traditionally boiled on the cob and served with butter, corn can be boiled or grilled on the barbecue in or out of the husk, or used as a base for chowders. Cooked corn kernels can be added to salads or stir-fried with rice dishes, or used in fritters and soups. Choose ears of corn with small pale kernels in even rows with pale silks. To husk corn, pull off the outer husks and silks; break or cut the stem if necessary.

FRUIT VEGETABLES

Botanically speaking, tomatoes, aubergines, sweet peppers and avocados are fruits, but are usually treated like vegetables in the kitchen. They each require different preparation and cooking techniques. Although each can be used as a principal ingredient, they can also be used as background or flavouring for other dishes.

Vine-ripened tomatoes have an intense perfume and superior flavour and texture – unfortunately, they are extremely fragile and do not travel well. They are only available during the summer and early fall. Greenhouse and hydroponic tomatoes (grown in water without soil) often look good but lack flavour, but they are available year round. Look for tomatoes grown for flavour. There are many varieties of tomato available, ranging from the giant "beefsteak" tomato to the thumbnail-sized cherry tomatoes so popular in salads.

PREPARING TOMATOES

Many recipes call for peeled, seeded and chopped tomatoes; this preparation is called *concasée* in French. It may seem complicated, but the result is worth it, providing a fresh intense tomato flavour with no skins or seeds.

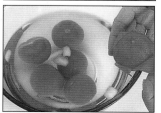

Core the tomatoes, then, using a small sharp knife, score the bottom of each tomato making an X just penetrating the skins. Drop the tomatoes into rapidly boiling water for 10–20 seconds, depending on their ripeness. Remove and refresh in ice water.

Remove the tomatoes from the water and peel off the skin, which will have begun to roll back.

Quarter each tomato and, using a small sharp knife, scrape out the seeds, or cut each tomato crosswise in half and squeeze out the seeds, using the knife to scrape out any remaining seeds. Slice or chop as recipe directs.

FRESH TOMATO SAUCE

1 Heat the oil in a large frying pan over medium heat. Add the onion and cook until soft and translucent, 5–8 minutes, stirring occasionally. Add the garlic and cook for 2 more minutes, until fragrant.

INGREDIENTS

1–2 tablespoons olive oil
1 onion, finely chopped
1–2 cloves garlic, finely chopped
450g (1lb) vine-ripened or plum
  tomatoes, peeled, seeded and
  chopped
$^1/_2$ teaspoon dried thyme
1 teaspoon sugar (optional)
1 tablespoon tomato purée
50ml (2 fl oz) water
2 tablespoons fresh chopped or
  torn basil leaves
salt and pepper

2 Add the tomatoes, dried thyme, sugar (if using) and tomato purée and water. Bring to the boil, then lower the heat and simmer for 25–30 minutes, stirring occasionally, to a purée-like consistency. Stir in the basil and season. Cook 5 more minutes until flavours blend. Season with salt and pepper.

GRILLING OR BARBECUING AUBERGINES

These large, plump, pear-shaped fruit vegetables, with shiny purple-black skins, are related to tomatoes. There are small round or elongated varieties available called Asian or Chinese aubergines. Both varieties have a pale greenish-grey bland flesh which absorbs flavours during cooking; they can be used interchangeably. Aubergines can be sliced crossways or lengthways, cubed or diced. It can be fried in oil (coated or uncoated) until tender, or braised in oil and stock or water.

PEPPERS

Sweet peppers are members of the capsicum family. They can be red, yellow, green, black, purple or orange. Pimientos are red peppers cultivated for roasting or canning: they are sweet with a bright reddish-orange colour. Sweet peppers add colour and flavour to many dishes, as well as making a delicious vegetable. Green peppers have a slightly grassy-bitter taste; yellow and red are the ripest and sweetest. Peppers can be cored and diced or sliced for salads and crudités, or fried, sautéed, grilled, or stuffed and baked.

PREPARING PEPPERS:
If the pepper is to be left whole for stuffing, cut off the stem end and scoop out the seeds with a spoon. Cut a very thin slice off the bottom end to allow the pepper to stand without wobbling. Prepare as the recipe directs. If the pepper is to be sliced or chopped, the flesh can be removed more easily.

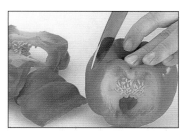

Trim the stem and bottom ends of the pepper, then cut off the 4 sides or "cheeks" from the centre cavity, and trim any remaining white ribs. You will have 4 "square" sides to slice or chop. Cut as recipe directs.

Alternatively, trim the stem and bottom ends off the pepper. Cut the pepper "circle" lengthways and open it out to a flat strip. Remove the core, ribs and seeds. Cut into strips or as recipe directs.

GOURDS AND SQUASHES

Squashes are a member of the gourd or *Cucurbitaceae* family, which contains hundreds of varieties around the world. Gourds tend to be found in warm regions such as Africa and India, but most squashes are native to the Americas. There are many varieties in a huge range of colours, shapes and sizes, but for the cook they can be divided into summer squash and winter squash.

PREPARING SUMMER SQUASH

Summer squash, characterized by the courgette, is soft-skinned with a mild, tender flesh, which can be eaten raw or lightly cooked by boiling, steaming or stir-frying.

Trim the ends, then slice or chop as the recipe directs. Fry in butter or oil over medium-high heat until tender, about 5 minutes.

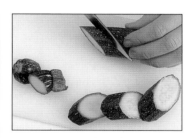

To make a courgette boat for stuffing, trim the stem end and cut in half lengthwise. Using a small sharp knife, score a 0.5-cm ($^1/_4$-in) border around the edge. Use a spoon to scoop out the seeds and flesh. Fill as recipe directs.

1 To prepare patty-pan squash, leave whole and trim ends, or trim and cut into halves or quarters.

2 To cook, steam over boiling water until just tender, 4–6 minutes. Alternatively, stir-fry in butter or oil 2–4 minutes until tender crisp and golden.

PREPARING WINTER SQUASH

Winter squash are picked when fully matured and so have thick hard skins with firm, compact, often darker-coloured, more flavourful flesh. After removing the large seeds, the flesh can be removed from the shell before or after cooking, but should not be eaten raw. It can be roasted, baked, steamed, sautéed or microwaved. It is ideal for puréeing and making soups or sweet pies such as pumpkin pie.

To prepare acorn, butternut or hubbard squash, cut in half. Then using a large spoon, scrape out seeds and fibres from the centre cavity of each half.

To remove the flesh before cooking, use a chef's knife to peel off the thick skin. To cook winter squash cubes, drop into boiling salted water and cook until tender, 8–10 minutes.

To purée winter squash, cook in boiling water until very tender 12–15 minutes. Drain well, then mash or process in a food processor until smooth. Add 2 tablespoons butter (or milk or cream) and a little nutmeg.

CUCUMBERS

Cucumbers, members of the gourd family, can be divided into two types, slicing and pickling. Although there are many varieties, the common green slicing cucumber is the one more often seen in supermarkets. This cucumber generally has a waxy coating which should be peeled before eating. The European hothouse cucumber is generally longer and thinner and has a thinner skin, so it is not necessary to peel it. It also has fewer seeds. The cool, refreshing taste and crunchy texture of cucumber makes it ideal in salads, in Middle Eastern dips such as *tzatziki*, and in Indian relishes and *raitas*.

CUCUMBER GARNISHES:
Use a garnishing knife to make deep lengthways ridges or use a vegetable peeler to remove alternate lengthways strips from the whole cucumber. Cut crossways in thin slices.

Cut each thin slice from the centre to the edge. Twist cut edges in the opposite direction and stand on their side.

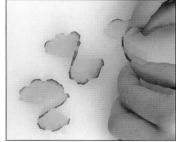

DICING:
Peel if recipe directs or if you like. Quarter the cucumber lengthways, then cut off the core triangle of seeds from each quarter. Cut into long strips, then into 5-cm (2-in) lengths, or dice or chop.

GREENS AND SALAD GREENS

Greens refer to a wide variety of leafy green vegetables, some of which can be eaten raw, but are often cooked. Greens are eaten in most countries around the world. Some greens, like mustard greens, sorrel, spinach, Swiss chard, dandelion, rocket, watercress and turnip greens, have a strong peppery flavour. Other greens like lettuces and salad greens are blander and are almost always eaten raw. Greens can be roughly divided into two categories: hearty greens (most often cooked) and salad greens (most often eaten raw), although the divisions are often blurred. All greens have a very high water content and shrink drastically when cooked; allow about 225g (8oz) per person if the greens are cooked.

HEARTY GREENS

Many of these sturdy, leafy greens (sometimes called pot herbs) can be eaten raw in salads when they are young and tender, but they are rarely found at this stage. Most are older and tougher, and need cooking to tenderize them and soften their often robust flavour.

SALAD GREENS

The major salad green, lettuce, can be divided into crisphead and butterhead, or soft-leaf, salads. Trim off the roots and wash well. Always dress salads gently at the last minute, so the dressing does not wilt the leaves.

PREPARING GREENS

Wash all greens well to remove any sand and grit. Immerse in a sink or bowl of cold water and soak 3–4 minutes, swishing the leaves around. Gently lift out of the water into a colander or strainer to drain. Repeat several times until no sand or grit remains on the bottom of the sink or bowl. Drain, shake well, and pile leaves in a colander.

Remove any large, tough stalks from spinach, kale, or other greens by gripping the leaf with one hand and pulling the stalk up and away from the leaf.

Separate the leaves from the stalks of Swiss chard by cutting the stalk out in a long V shape.

To shred bok choy or chard leaves, stack the leaves and roll together, then slice crossways into thick or thin shreds as the recipe directs.

Cut the stalk into 2.5-cm (1-in) pieces and tear or shred the leaves; cook each separately as the leaves cook more quickly than the stalks. The leaf and stalk of young tender bok choy may be left together as the cooking time is very short. Separate from the root and trim if they are still attached.

COOKING GREENS

To cook spinach, put the leaves in a saucepan with just the water which clings to the leaves from washing. Set over medium heat and cook gently until just wilted, 2–3 minutes, or stir-fry in a little butter or oil until wilted, 1–2 minutes. To blanch, dip into boiling water for 30 seconds.

If using cooked spinach or other greens in another preparation, such as creamed spinach or a braised dish, transfer into a sieve and press out as much liquid as possible with a wooden spoon. Use leaves whole or chop as recipe directs.

Stir-fry bok choy or Swiss chard in a little butter or oil until just wilted and tender, 2–6 minutes. For an oriental flavour, season with a little soy sauce and a drop or two of sesame oil.

CABBAGE AND BRASSICAS

Cabbage, a member of the Brassica family, is one of the oldest vegetables cultivated by man. There are many kinds of cabbage, mostly characterized by round heads of compact leaves, though some are flattened, elongated, or more loosely packed. Cabbage is generally a cold weather vegetable, inexpensive, widely available, and easy to prepare and cook, which may explain its wide use in many cultures. It can be eaten raw as in coleslaw, pickled as in sauerkraut, or cooked in a wide variety of ways. Do not overcook cabbage, as it becomes soggy and has a very unpleasant smell. Look for cabbages heavy for their size, discarding any tough outer leaves.

White cabbage, sometimes called round or Dutch cabbage, is the most common. Usually trimmed of its darker, tough outer leaves, it has a firm, pale green head and solid core with a robust flavour. It can be shredded for crisp salads or coleslaw, stir-fried, braised, boiled, simmered in soups, or stuffed. This is the cabbage used for sauerkraut. Savoy cabbage or curly cabbage has slightly looser leaves and a purple tinge, and is more delicate in flavour. Red cabbage has a brilliant purple colour and a slightly sweeter taste. It needs a slightly longer cooking time than white cabbage and is often braised with onion and apple to accompany duck or game. An acid such as vinegar is usually added to set the colour. For this reason a little vinegar is added to braised cabbage as well as the apple. A little sugar usually complements the acid, giving it a sweet and sour flavour.

Chinese cabbage, sometimes called Napa cabbage, has pale greenish-yellow elongated leaves. It is milder in flavour than white cabbage, can be eaten raw or cooked, and is an ingredient in many Chinese stir-fries.

BRUSSEL SPROUTS

The Brussel sprout is a cool season crop, belonging to the cabbage family, and closely related to cauliflower, broccoli, kale, collards, etc. Like cauliflower, it thrives best in a cool humid climate. The edible portion of this crop is the "bud" or small cabbage-like head which grows in the axils of each leaf. Occasionally the tops are used as greens. These miniature cabbages originated in Belgium where they are grown on thick stalks. Rarely eaten raw, they have a strong, nutty flavour which goes well with game, duck and other rich meats. They are sometimes braised with chestnuts and accompany the Christmas turkey. Boil or steam until just tender, 7–10 minutes.

PREPARING SPROUTS

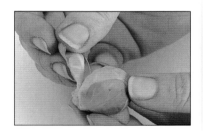

To prepare Brussel sprouts, remove any loose or slightly yellow outer leaves. With a sharp knife, score an X in the base for more even cooking.

PREPARING CABBAGE

To prepare cabbage, cut in half and cut out the core in a V shape. If whole leaves are needed for stuffing, pull them apart, detaching them intact from the stem, then blanch as for spinach leaves, increasing the time slightly; refresh in cold water.

To shred, set one half cut side down, and cut crosswise into thick or thin slices as the recipe directs.

BROCCOLI AND CAULIFLOWER

Members of the cabbage family, broccoli and cauliflower both have tightly grouped flower buds coming from a single stalk. They can be eaten raw in salads and crudité platters or cooked in a variety of ways, whole or separated into florets. Boil or steam florets until tender, 5–10 minutes.

CAULIFLOWER:
To prepare cauliflower, remove the outer green leaves and the core from the stem end. Break the cauliflower into pieces, then break off florets.

BROCCOLI:
To prepare broccoli, trim the thick woody stem and break off small florets. Alternatively, leave the stalk longer, but trim it. Split the head of broccoli into quarters and trim the tough outer skin from the outside of the base.

GARLIC CAULIFLOWER

INGREDIENTS

1 small head of cauliflower
1 tablespoon virgin olive oil
2 large cloves garlic, minced
1 tablespoon toasted sesame seeds
Dash paprika (optional)
Pepper to taste (optional)

1 In a large pot, bring 2 quarts (2.25 litres) of water to the boil.
2 Trim cauliflower and break into florets. Drop into boiling water and cook about 2 minutes.
3 Drain in a colander.
4 In a large, non-stick frying pan, heat oil and toast garlic. Add cauliflower and sesame seeds and saute for 1 minute.
5 Dust with paprika and pepper before serving (optional).

MUSHROOMS AND TRUFFLES

Mushrooms, members of the fungi family, are one of the oldest foods eaten by man. There are many different varieties which vary in size, shape, colour and flavour, but all have a central stalk with an umbrella-shaped cap.

There are two types of mushroom, cultivated and wild, and most of them are prepared and cooked in similar ways. The cultivated mushroom, or common white mushroom, has been successfully produced since the late 1800s. Very young white closed-cap mushrooms are called button mushrooms. They are mild in flavour and widely available year round. Flat mushrooms, sometimes called field mushrooms, are ideal for grilling. A growing number of previously wild varieties are now being cultivated. Mushrooms like the shitake, enokitake (enoki or pinhead), cloud ears and oyster are all now widely available.

Wild mushrooms are found all over the world, most frequently in late summer and autumn, in many woods and fields providing the perfect conditions. The flavour is intensely earthy, and they should always be cooked before eating. Many mushrooms can be dangerous, so do not pick or gather wild mushrooms unless you are accompanied by an expert mycologist or guide, and always purchase wild mushrooms from a reputable dealer. Wild mushrooms such as morels, boletus (also called cepe or porcini) parasols, wood hedgehogs, blewits, chanterelles, horn of plenty and chicken of the wood are all expensive, but so highly flavoured that a little goes a long way. Some of the wild varieties are available dried: morels, boletus (cepe or porcini), shitake, matsutake and cloud ear can all be purchased dried and are easily reconstituted. The most famous fungi is the truffle. This pungent, black treasure is really a tuber, sniffed out of the oak forests of the French Perigord (black) and Italian Piedmont (white) by pigs or dogs. The fresh variety is prohibitively expensive, but they are available in jars, and although they lose much of their aroma, even a small amount can add intense flavour to foods.

Wrap fresh mushrooms loosely in paper towels and refrigerate up to 3 days. Do not store in plastic bags because the moisture will cause rapid deterioration.

PREPARING MUSHROOMS

Cultivated mushrooms should not be washed before using. Use a mushroom brush or soft toothbrush to brush off any earth or grit, or wipe with damp kitchen paper. If they are very earthy or sandy, plunge quickly into a bowl of cold water, lift out and drain; dry immediately. Trim the stalks.

Wild mushrooms are often very sandy and do need washing. Plunge into several changes of cold water, lift out and drain. Trim off any woody stems and tough outer edges. Morels sometimes need soaking to draw out the sand.

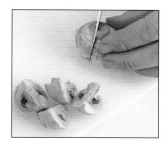

To prepare mushrooms, clean them and trim the stems. Quarter large mushrooms or slice as recipe directs. Use a stainless steel knife as other materials can discolour mushrooms. Sprinkle with a little lemon juice to prevent darkening if preparing ahead or chopping a large quantity.

COOKING MUSHROOMS

Heat butter or oil in a frying pan over medium-high heat until very hot, but not smoking. Add the mushrooms, and sauté or stir-fry 3–4 minutes until golden and tender. Continue cooking until any liquid evaporates

Open cap or field mushrooms can be brushed with butter or oil and grilled 10cm (4in) from the heat until browned and tender, 6–8 minutes. Baste occasionally.

THE ONION FAMILY

These strong flavoured, aromatic vegetables are members of the lily family. Onions, spring onions, leeks, shallots and garlic are sometimes used as vegetables, but are most often used as flavourings in other dishes. Chives are the only true herb in the onion family. Onions vary in colour, size, texture and flavour and are used in every cuisine around the world.

Onions and their relatives can be used raw or cooked. Their flavour varies from mild and sweet to pungently strong. Large, mild varieties of the stronger common yellow onion, or globe onion, are named after their place of origin: the Spanish Valencia, Hawaiian Maui, the Bermuda, the Vidalia and the Walla Walla from the southern American states. These sweet onions are best sliced raw in salads or on sandwiches and hamburgers. They are also excellent for stuffing or grilling on the barbecue. Large white onions are slightly milder than yellow ones. Red onions are sweet and best eaten raw.

Pearl onions, sometimes called pickling onions or silverskins, are harvested when they are about 2.5cm (1in) in diameter. Boiling onions are slightly larger, and cocktail onions are tiny white onions kept small by compact planting, which inhibits their growth. Baby onions are available peeled and frozen, and are often used in stews and braised meat dishes. Long spring onions or green onions are immature yellow onions grown for their milder flavour. Leeks are the mildest and sweetest of the onion family, frequently used to flavour soups and stocks.

PREPARING ONIONS

Use a small, sharp knife to cut the stem end and peel off the papery skin; leave the root end intact to help hold the onion together. Trim the root ends of spring onions and remove wilting leaves.

1 Cut the onion in half lengthways. Set each half cut side down on a cutting board. With a sharp knife make a series of vertical cuts, cutting just to, but not through, the root. Then make a series of horizontal cuts from the stem in towards the root.

2 Cut the onion crossways, allowing it to fall into dice. If you want a finer dice, continue chopping the onion, using a rocking motion with the knife against the board.

ONION RINGS:
To cut onion rings, steady the peeled onion against the board and cut crossways into thick or thin slices. Alternatively, halve the onion, set it cut side down, and cut crossways into half rings.

CREAMED ONIONS

INGREDIENTS

12 small white onions, peeled
50g (2oz) butter
25g (1oz) flour
dash of black pepper
pinch of nutmeg
250ml (8 fl oz) milk

Peel onions. Place in boiling water and cook for 15–20 minutes until tender but not overdone. Drain and place aside. In a separate pan melt butter, whisk in flour, pepper, and nutmeg and cook for 1 minute. Add milk and cook until thickened. Stir in onions and serve warm.

PREPARING LEEKS

Leeks are famous for hiding sand and grit between their leaves and need thorough washing.

Discard any tough or yellow outer leaves and trim the root end. Trim some of the green top, as the recipe directs, and, unless using whole, slit the leek in half or quarters from the top into the white part. Plunge leeks into cold water down to the root, shaking to loosen any grit. Repeat if necessary. Slice, chop or julienne as recipe directs. If using whole, do not slit; soak in cold water, shaking to remove any grit.

PREPARING ONIONS AND LEEKS

Onions should be cooked slowly in butter or oil until soft and transparent. This method, called sweating, brings out their natural sweetness. If they are cooked too quickly and allowed to brown or scorch, they will become bitter. Leeks can be sautéed for use in other dishes, or cooked quickly.

Heat 1 tablespoon butter or oil in a saucepan or skillet over medium heat. Add chopped or sliced onions and cook gently, stirring occasionally, or braise slowly over very low heat, covered, for 30 minutes until lightly golden.

To sauté sliced or chopped leeks, heat 15–25g ($^1/_2$–1oz) butter in a large frying pan over medium-high heat. Add the leeks and stir-fry until bright green and just tender, 3–4 minutes. Small whole spring onions can be stir-fried the same way.

STALKS AND SHOOTS

Stalks and shoots are vegetable plant stems which contain a high percentage of cellulose fibre. These vegetables – asparagus, celery and artichokes (an edible thistle) – tend to be crisp when raw and highly aromatic when cooked – most have been eaten for hundreds of years.

Asparagus can range from pencil thin to jumbo, extra-thick spears. Fresh-tasting green asparagus is most popular. The thick, white asparagus preferred by the French and Belgians is milder and slightly softer. Common celery is used as a flavouring in soups, stocks and stews, but can be eaten raw in salads, used for dipping, or gently braised. Fennel, sometimes called by its Italian name *finocchio*, is a Mediterranean plant with a fresh, crunchy texture and anise flavour, ideal for salads and crudités, braising or stir-frying. Tender, young artichokes can be cooked and eaten whole, and are very popular in Italian cooking. In large globe artichokes, the choke, or flower, must be discarded.

PREPARING AND COOKING WHOLE ARTICHOKES

Always use a stainless steel knife to prepare artichokes, and rub all cut surfaces with lemon juice to prevent discoloration.

1 Snap off the stalk close to the base, pulling out any fibres which would extend into the bottom, then trim the base with a knife so it sits flat. Cut off the pointed top and, using kitchen scissors, trim the leaves to remove spines and any brown edges. Separate the leaves and rinse under cold running water. The artichoke is ready to be cooked whole.

2 Boil a large saucepan of salted water. Add the juice of 1 lemon or 3–4 tablespoons vinegar and the artichoke, upside down, and cover with a heatproof plate or wet cloth to keep it submerged. Simmer until tender, when the stem end can be pierced with a fork or knife tip, 15–25 minutes, depending on size. Drain upside down and cool slightly.

3 To remove the choke, first grasp the central cone of leaves with your fingers and twist and lift out; reserve the cone of leaves. Using a teaspoon, separate the leaves and scrape out the hairy choke and discard.
4 Replace the reserved cone of leaves, upside down in the centre, and fill it with a favourite dipping.

PREPARING AND COOKING ASPARAGUS

Very thin, tender asparagus only needs washing and trimming the stalk ends. Thicker asparagus should be peeled to remove the stringy outer layers and woody stems.

To cook, fill a large skillet with 2.5cm (1in) water and $^1/_2$ teaspoon salt. Bring to the boil over medium-high heat. Add the asparagus and simmer 3–4 minutes until tender. Asparagus spears can be also cooked upright in tall asparagus steamers, or stir-fried.

PREPARING AND COOKING CELERY

Celery benefits from lightly peeling to remove the coarsest strings from the outside of the stalks. Snap the end of a celery stalk, but do not separate it completely; pull off with the strings attached. Alternatively, peel each stalk with a vegetable peeler.

To braise slices, simmer with 15g ($^1/_2$oz) butter and 2–3 tablespoons stock or water, 2–3 minutes, until just tender. Cover celery hearts with about 225ml (8 fl oz) water and 1 tablespoon butter, and simmer about 20 minutes.

GRAINS AND PULSES

Grains and pulses should be kept as fresh as possible. Good, bright colour, plump texture and a fresh aroma are a good sign. As they age, both grains and pulses require longer cooking. Store them in a cool, dry place in airtight containers.

RICE AND OTHER GRAINS

The harvesting process dehydrates grains, so they must be cooked in a generous amount of liquid to reabsorb moisture and soften. Water is the most accessible, but stock can be used for savoury dishes, while milk is usual for breakfast porridge and rice puddings. Timings vary for different grains, tempered by their age and dryness. Whole grains will need longer cooking than polished or refined varieties. Most grains should be cooked *al dente*, tender but with a slight firmness on the inside; whole grains are a little chewier. Some – such as wild rice – burst when done, but most should hold their shape. Grains can be boiled, steamed, baked or cooked as pilaf but whatever method you choose, allow the cooked grain to stand, covered, for about 5 minutes. This allows the individual grains to contract, much like letting meat rest. To separate the grains, toss lightly with a fork.

Amaranth is a tall plant with very broad leaves which produces many thousands of tiny seeds. Both the leaves and the seeds are edible. The amaranth is closely related to pigweed, spinach and beetroot.

Quinoa is a cereal grain from Peru, which is closely related to the amaranth. The seed of the quinoa is about 3mm (0.2in) in diameter and is cooked and eaten much like oatmeal.

Spelt is a sub-species of common wheat and is one of the oldest grains to be cultivated. It is finding renewed popularity with consumers.

Amaranth

Long grain rice

Quinoa

Wild rice

A DICTIONARY OF RICE

There are hundreds of kinds of rice, most defined by the size of the grain, some by their origins. Different varieties need different styles of cooking and result in an assortment of flavours and textures. Some long-grain white rice is converted: that is, partially steamed to force nutrients from the outer bran into the endosperm so they are maintained when the rice is husked.

Long-grain rice cooks dry and fluffy, providing tender, separate grains. It is 4 to 5 times as long as it is wide. *Carolina* is a long-grain variety grown in the southern states of America. *Basmati*, another long-grain rice is sometimes called "the Champagne of rice." Highly prized for its exotic perfume, it is a staple of Indian cooking, requiring rinsing before use. *Pecan rice* is a long-grain brown rice variety with the flavour of pecans.

Medium-grain rice, such as *arborio*, is slightly rounder and absorbs a little more liquid than long-grain varieties, producing a slightly more moist, stickier result. But it can be used as long-grain rice.

Sticky rice or glutinous rice is a medium- to short-grain rice used in Chinese and Japanese cooking because it is easier to eat with chopsticks.

Thai fragrant rice has a special perfume, and its young, tender grains are much prized by the Thais and Vietnamese.

Wild rice is an aquatic grass which grows along rivers and lakes on the Canadian-American border. The long, thin, black grains have a nutty flavour and chewy texture. It is often mixed with white rice to defray the cost – it is very expensive. It takes 15 to 20 minutes longer than white rice to cook and absorbs about four times its volume in liquid.

Other grains Many other grains can be cooked and eaten like rice; some may absorb more water than white rice. Follow directions on the package.

Spelt (or Farro) is known as a hulled wheat. This grain is very nutritious, with high energy characteristics. This incredibly creamy and delicious grain cooks in just 20 to 30 minutes, and makes a wonderful risotto.

COOKING RICE AND OTHER GRAINS

TO BOIL: Bring a large pot of water to the boil (about 4 times the amount of water to rice or other grain). Gradually add rice (or other grain) so water continues to boil. Stir once, and continue to boil until it tests tender. Drain in a colander and rinse with hot water.

THE ABSORPTION METHOD: Put water or stock (usually $1^1/_2$ times the amount of rice) in a medium saucepan and bring to the boil. Add rice and bring back to the boil. Stir, then steam, covered, 18–20 minutes, until water is completely absorbed and rice is tender (about 15 minutes more for brown rice).

TO BAKE: Put the measured rice in an ovenproof baking dish. Pour in $1^1/_2$ times the amount of boiling water or stock. Stir and cover tightly. Bake in a 180°C (350°F/Gas 4) oven for about 25 minutes, until the water has been absorbed and rice is tender. (Cook brown rice about 15 minutes longer.)

TO STEAM: Line a steamer with dampened muslin. Spread the rice evenly over the surface and place over a pan of simmering water. Cover and steam about 20 minutes, until tender.

THE PILAF METHOD: Heat a small amount of butter or oil in a saucepan over medium heat. Stir in the rice and cook 2 minutes, until it becomes opaque. Add $1^1/_2$ times the amount of water or stock to rice. Season with salt and pepper, and stir once. Bring to the boil and cover. Reduce heat and cook 18 to 20 minutes, until tender.

COOKING BULGAR (CRACKED WHEAT): TABBOULEH SALAD

Bulgar is a type of cracked wheat with a nutty flavour, which cooks to a light fluffy texture. Highly nutritious, it is made by steaming wheat berries before drying and cracking them into tiny pieces.

This Middle Eastern favourite can be simmered or cooked by the pilaf method, or steamed like rice. It only needs to be soaked before it is used in tabbouleh, a herb salad of parsley, mint, bulgar and tomatoes.

INGREDIENTS

115g (4oz) bulgar wheat
1 medium red onion, finely chopped
150g (5oz) seeded and chopped tomatoes (peeled if you like)
5 tablespoons chopped Italian flat-leaf parsley (continental)
5 tablespoons chopped fresh mint
125ml (4 fl oz) virgin olive oil
50ml (2 fl oz) freshly squeezed lemon juice

1 To soak: rinse under cold running water. Turn into a large bowl and cover with twice as much water as bulgar. Allow it to stand 1 hour until plump and tender. Add more water if necessary. Drain if too much liquid is added. Fluff with a fork to separate grains.

2 Stir in the onion, chopped tomatoes, chopped herbs, oil and lemon juice or vinegar. Season with the salt and black pepper. Garnish with mint leaves and lemon wedges. Serve with black olives. (The salad should look very green, not beige.)

PREPARING AND COOKING COUSCOUS

Couscous is not really a grain, but a tiny pasta. This North African staple is made from semolina (durum wheat), which was traditionally hand-rolled into "grains" that were dampened and coated with flour. This slightly enlarges the grains and helps to keep them separate during cooking. Most of the couscous now available is processed mechanically, replacing the labour-intensive procedure. It simply needs a short soaking, then steaming. This is called quick-cooking couscous.

Couscous is the name of a famous North African stew simmered in a special steamer or *couscoussière*. Couscous makes a delicious stuffing for poultry and can be soaked and used like bulgar for a tabbouleh-style salad.

1 Put the couscous in a large strainer and rinse under cold running water until the water runs clear. Turn into a bowl and add enough cold water to cover by 1cm (¹/₂in). Allow to stand about 30 minutes. Drain again. (If the couscous is being used for stuffing, proceed as the recipe directs.)

2 To serve the couscous as the main accompaniment, line a colander or flat steamer with dampened muslin and set aside. Rub the drained couscous between your fingers to remove any lumps and put in the colander. Set over a pan of boiling water (or the stew) and steam, uncovered, for about 30 minutes. Serve with the traditional stew or other meats and vegetables.

BUSY COOKS

QUICK COOKING COUSCOUS
Put 15g (¹/₂oz) butter or oil in a saucepan with 350ml (12 fl oz) water or stock. Season with salt, pepper, and any other desired spices or herbs. Bring to the boil and gradually stir in 115g (4oz) couscous. Return to the boil and remove from the heat. Cover and allow to stand about 10 minutes. Fluff with a fork before serving.

POLENTA: COOKING POLENTA

Polenta is coarsely ground cornmeal cooked in water or stock to a mushy consistency. Stirred with butter, oil, and/or cheese, and sometimes served with a tomato sauce, it is a popular northern Italian side dish with roast meats, sausages and stews. It can also be chilled, sliced and fried or baked. Polenta must be watched and stirred constantly as it cooks to a thick, creamy mass.

INGREDIENTS

900ml (1¹/₂ pints) water
1¹/₂ teaspoons salt
150g (5oz) polenta
50g (2oz) unsalted butter
40–50g (1¹/₂–2oz) Parmesan cheese,
    freshly grated

1 Put water and salt in a deep, heavy-bottom saucepan and bring to the boil. Gradually add polenta in a steady stream, whisking constantly. Stir in half the butter.

2 Reduce heat to low and stir constantly, using a wooden spoon, 15–20 minutes until thickened. The mixture will begin to pull away from the side of the pan. Remove from heat and stir in cheese and remaining butter. Serve immediately as a hot accompaniment.

3 To serve in slices, proceed as above, omitting the butter and cheese, if you like. Then pour the hot polenta into an oiled loaf, cake or Swiss-roll tin, smoothing the top evenly. Cool completely, and chill until firm. Use broiled polenta slices as a base for tomato or meat sauces or garlicky sautéed mushrooms.

CORN AND CORNMEAL

In many parts of the world, especially in the United States, corn rivals wheat as the most important grain. There are many varieties of corn, including a blue one that originated with Native Americans which has a sweet, earthy taste. It is usually ground like flour and made into tortillas and corn chips.

Cornmeal is finely ground from dried wheat or yellow corn. Most of it is ground from the kernel after the hull and germ are removed. It is a staple in many parts of the world. It is eaten boiled (4 parts water to 1 part cornmeal) as a hot breakfast cereal with butter or syrup, or cooled, sliced, and fried as a side dish. It is used in a wide variety of puddings, cornbreads, muffins and tortillas. It also makes a crispy coating for fish. It can be stored for one year in a cool, dry place. *Cornstarch* is a finely powdered starch ground from corn kernels. It is used as a thickener for sauces, especially in Chinese recipes. It can help "soften" some hard flours; use it to replace 1–2 tablespoons from 150g (5oz) of plain flour to make delicate pastries or shortbread.

Hominy is the dried kernel of hulled corn. It is softened first by soaking, then by long cooking in milk. It is either sold as kernels or ground into hominy grits.

Grits are ground hominy, a fine, white cereal cooked in water to a mushy consistency for breakfast dishes and side dishes. It is very popular in the south.

PULSES

Pulses, which include peas, beans and lentils, are the edible seeds of pod plants. Most commonly sold dried, they are second only to grains as the world's most important foodstuff. High in protein and carbohydrates, they are indispensable in a vegetarian diet. Combined with grains, they form a complete protein. This duo forms the basis of many national dishes, from Mexican beans and rice to Italian pasta and bean soup.

BEAN GLOSSARY

There is a tremendous range of dried beans, peas and lentils, varying in size, colour and shape. Most need at least 4 hours soaking, but can be left overnight to save time. Soaking is not necessary for lentils or split peas, although it will shorten their cooking time.

Aduki beans A small, sweet, reddish bean used in Asia and called "King of beans" in Japan.

Black beans Also called "turtle beans", these smooth, shiny little black beans, which keep their shape well, are popular for soups and stews.

Black-eyed peas These small, oval, cream-coloured beans have a black dot on one side with a small cream dot in the centre.

Borlotti beans This medium-size Italian bean is kidney-shaped with a reddish-pink colour and tan stripes, often used in salads.

Lima beans Similar to butter beans, these flat, oval beans are pale green and cook to a soft tender consistency.

Cannellini Also called the *fazolia* bean, this bean is an important ingredient in minestrone.

Garbanzo beans Also called chickpeas or *ceci* in Italian. Roundish, wrinkled, pea-shaped beans, they need long soaking and cooking. They are popular in Middle Eastern dishes.

Dried peas These round field peas are a staple in the Mediterranean. They vary in colour from blue-grey to brown-black.

Split peas are dried peas, split in half when their seed coat peels away. Yellow split peas are milder than green ones; they are also sweeter and less starchy than whole peas, and are the main ingredient in Ham and Pea Soup.

Aduki beans

Garbanzo beans

Butter beans

Black-eyed beans or peas

Borlotti beans

BEAN GLOSSARY CONTINUED

Flageolet beans These mild, pale green beans often complement lamb in France.

Haricot beans Also known as the Great Northern bean with a mild flavour and mealy texture, which holds its shape well. Widely used, it is slightly larger than the navy bean, or the pearl haricot.

Kidney beans Smooth, shiny, kidney-shaped beans can be red, white or black. Most common is the hearty red kidney bean or red bean used in Chilli con carne.

Lentils The smaller the better, these green, red or brown flat, dried seeds, need little or no soaking. The deep, greenish grey-blue Puy lentil keeps its shape as a hot accompaniment or in salads. The red or yellow lentil is used in Indian *dal*.

Pinto beans Pretty beige, oval beans speckled with pink, these small beans can be substituted for red kidney beans.

Soya beans These small, round Asian beans can be black or beige. Rich in carbohydrates, they form the base of many other products, from flours to milk to soy sauce.

Dried peas

Lentils

Haricot beans

Soya beans

Red kidney beans

SOAKING AND COOKING PULSES

With the exception of lentils and split peas, dried pulses need soaking to shorten the cooking time, make them more digestible, and prevent splitting. Garbanzo and soya beans are especially dense and need slightly longer soaking.

1 Pick over the beans or peas and rinse under cold running water. Put them in a large bowl, cover by at least 2.5cm (1in) cold water, and soak for 6 to 8 hours or overnight. Drain and rinse well.

2 Alternatively, put pulses in a large pot, cover with cold water, and bring to the boil. Boil for 2 minutes, remove from heat, cover, and stand for 1 hour. Drain and rinse.

3 Put beans in a large saucepan or flameproof casserole and cover with cold water (3 parts water to 1 part pulses). Bring to the boil over medium-high heat. Boil rapidly for 10 minutes. Simmer 45 minutes to 1 hour, depending on the type and age of the pulse.

4 When the beans are cooked, the interior should be soft but the skin firm.

BEAN KNOW-HOW

Most pulses need to be boiled rapidly for the first ten minutes to remove toxins on the skin. Reduce the heat and simmer gently for the remainder of the cooking time. Lentils and split peas do not need this treatment. Simply bring to the boil, reduce the heat and simmer.

CHILI CON CARNE

This dish can be made either on top of the stove or in the oven. The oven should be preheated to 170°C (325°F/Gas 4).

1 Put the onions and garlic in the food processor and process until finely chopped. Transfer to a flameproof casserole then fry in a little olive oil until softened. Add the chilli powder, fresh chilli, cumin and a little seasoning. Then add the ground beef and continue to cook, stirring, until it has browned. Process the sun-dried tomatoes in the food processor with enough oil from the jar to loosen into a paste. Add these to the beef with the tomatoes, cinnamon stick, and 250ml (8 fl oz) of water.

INGREDIENTS

2 medium onions
1 clove garlic
olive oil
2 teaspoons chilli powder
1 fresh red chilli, seeded and finely chopped
1 teaspoon ground cumin (or crushed cumin seeds)
sea salt and freshly ground black pepper
450g (1lb) ground beef
250g (8oz) sun-dried tomatoes in olive oil
2 400-g (1-lb) tins chopped tomatoes
$1/2$ stick cinnamon
2 400-g) (1-lb) tins red kidney beans, drained

2 Bring to the boil, cover, then either turn down the heat and cook for $1^{1}/_{2}$ hours or put in the oven for about $1^{1}/_{2}$ hours. Add the kidney beans 30 minutes before the end of the cooking time – they are already cooked and need only warming up. Serve over rice.

FRUIT

The vast range of fruit available provides endless opportunities for even inexperienced cooks to make healthy and appetizing dishes and snacks. Easy to peel and prepare, fruit can make an unusual and exotic addition to your repertoire.

FRUIT

Fruits offer the cook a tremendous variety of colour, flavour and texture. Most commonly eaten out of hand as a snack, fruit appears in meals throughout the day; from sliced bananas on breakfast cereals to apple pie for evening dessert. Used in starters, salads, soups and main courses, fruit also makes the perfect partner with cheese. It forms the basis of pickles, relishes, jams and, of course, desserts. It can be served raw, poached, sautéed, battered, deep-fried, boiled, baked or puréed. It is used to make mousses, sauces, pies, sorbets and ice creams.

CHOOSING AND RIPENING FRUIT

Choose fruit which is heavy for its size. It should be fragrant and fresh smelling, yielding slightly when pressed with the fingertips near the stalk end. Allow unripened fruit to ripen at room temperature, then refrigerate. Buy only as much as you need because ripe fruit cannot be stored for very long. To speed up the ripening process, place fruit in a brown paper bag.

CLEANING FRUIT

Fruits with edible skins, such as apples, pears, plums, nectarines and grapes, should be washed before eating. However, delicate berries should be washed *only if necessary*. Some fruits, like apples and lemons, are waxed; they should be scrubbed with water before grating, julienning or eating unpeeled.

PREVENTING DISCOLORATION

Fruits such as apples, pears, peaches, bananas and avocados quickly turn brown when sliced. This reaction of enzymes to the air can be slowed down by rubbing the cut surfaces with an acid, such as lemon, lime, orange or grapefruit juice.

FRUIT TYPES

Fruit can be roughly divided into eight categories: pomes, citrus, berries, grapes, drupes (or stone fruits), melons, exotic and tropical fruits. Pomes are thin-skinned tree fruits, with firm flesh and a central core containing seeds. Apples, pears, crab apples and quinces are pomes. Drupes are thin-skinned fruit with a hard stone or seed in the middle, such as apricots, peaches and plums.

TROPICAL AND EXOTIC FRUITS

Thanks to air transportation, tropical fruits are now widely available. Most are eaten raw, although some are used in cooked desserts or puréed for use in sorbets and ice creams.

Bananas Yellow bananas are peeled before eating. They can be sliced and added to fruit salad, trifle or pudding. Mashed banana adds flavour and moisture to cakes, quickbreads and muffins.

Pineapple is one of the most versatile tropical fruits. It can be cut into rings, spears and chunks, or halves of the fruit hollowed into boats and filled with other fruits. Fresh pineapple contains an enzyme, bromelin, which breaks down gelatine, so do not use it in gelatine-based desserts. Canned or cooked pineapple may be used instead.

Paw paw (papaya) can be prepared like melon; cut lengthways, scoop out the black seeds and any fibres, and serve, or cut into wedges and peel like melon wedges. Natural papain, contained in papaya juice, can be used to tenderize meats but it, too, cannot be used in gelatine-based desserts.

Kiwi fruit This sweet yet tart fruit has a bright green flesh and tiny black seeds. Kiwi also breaks down gelatine and prevents gelling.

Passion fruit Sometimes called grenadilla, this dark,

purple-brown, wrinkled fruit has orangy-flavoured pulp and black seeds. The strong flavour is ideal for use in custards, sauces and creams.

Avocado This popular fruit can be eaten on its own, sliced for use in salads, mashed for dips, used in soups or mousses, or lightly baked.

Mangoes These highly perfumed fruits are very juicy and can be prepared in several ways.

Figs Figs can be lightly baked, used in compotes, or eaten raw.

Pomegranates The seeds of the pomegranate symbolized fertility in many ancient cultures, and its juice is still a popular Mediterranean drink.

Avocado

Pomegranate

Figs

COOKING FRUIT: POACHING

Although fruit is most frequently eaten in the hand or in fresh fruit salads and desserts, it forms the base of many cooked desserts. Fruits can be poached, baked, grilled and puréed, and are often used to garnish side dishes.

Sugar and lemon are used to bring out the flavour in both uncooked fruit and in cooked fruit preparations. Poached fruit can be served on its own, or as part of a fruit compôte. Cook in a simple sugar syrup flavoured with vanilla, lemon or orange zest, cinnamon, cloves or wine, as the recipe directs.

1 Make a simple sugar syrup by heating 500ml (18 fl oz) water with 250g (8oz) sugar in a saucepan over low heat until the sugar dissolves. Then boil for about 1 minute until the syrup looks crystal clear. Peel and core the fruit. Gently lower into the hot syrup and cover with a piece of baking parchment (this helps to keep the fruit immersed in the liquid).

2 Gently simmer until the fruit feels tender when pierced with the point of a knife. Timing varies, depending on the fruit used and the degree of ripeness. Remove from the heat and cool in the poaching liquid.

DEEP-FRYING FRUIT

Some fruits can be deep-fried, but most fruit pieces are dipped in a batter before frying. The "fritters" are then sprinkled with icing sugar before serving.

175

PASTA, NOODLES, AND DUMPLINGS

Although pasta has been a household ingredient for years, it became seriously trendy in the early 1980s. Served in every restaurant and widely available in supermarkets, Italian delicatessens and speciality stores, pasta is probably one of the world's most popular foods. Noodles are increasingly popular, especially with the explosion of interest in foods from the Far East. Dumplings are a traditional, warming and filling accompaniment to stews and desserts.

PASTA

Made from an unleavened combination of flour and liquid (either water or eggs) pasta is a versatile, inexpensive, nutritious food, a well-known staple since ancient times throughout Italy, the Middle East and Asia. After industrial production of pasta began in Naples, Italy, during the 18th century, the popularity of pasta began to spread worldwide.

There are two basic types of pasta: dried and fresh. When buying dried pasta, look for the words "durum wheat", "pure semolina" or "pasta di semola di grano duro" on the package. Dried pasta is available in countless shapes and sizes, as well as in many flavours, such as spinach, beetroot, herb and garlic; they are almost always known by their Italian names. Dried packaged "egg noodles" are one of the few widely available dried egg noodles. Dried pasta keeps indefinitely if stored in a cool, dry place.

Fresh pasta has become popular and very chic in the last few years. Made from flour, eggs and sometimes a little oil and salt for flavour, it is rolled out by hand or machine, then cut into noodles, shaped into bows, spirals or other forms, or filled with a stuffing. Fresh pasta is usually made with a strong flour or a special pasta flour, as home-made pasta made with semolina is almost impossible to roll out thinly and is difficult to handle. It can be made by hand or in a food processor. A pasta machine is invaluable for kneading, rolling and cutting homemade pasta.

PASTA GLOSSARY

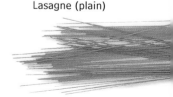

Lasagne (plain)

Tricolor fusilli

Pipe rigate

Whole wheat spaghetti

PASTA GLOSSARY CONTINUED

There are hundreds of pasta shapes, both dried and fresh.

Lasagne Broad noodles at least 5cm (2in) wide, available dried or fresh. The cooked noodle is layered with meat or tomato sauce, cheese and vegetables, or seafood, and baked in a casserole.

Fusilli tricolor Corkscrew-shaped noodles about 5cm (2in) long (they can be spaghetti-length).

Farfalle Butterfly-shaped noodles about 5cm (2in) long and 2cm ($^3/_4$in) wide. Pinched in at the middle.

Pipe rigate Small, short, ridged pasta shapes.

Conchiglie Small, shell shaped.

Penne rigate Sometimes called quills, 5cm (2in) long ridged tubes cut on the diagonal.

Egg campanelle Use with a chunky sauce.

Tagliatelle (paglia e fieno). A ribbon-like flat noodle about 0.5cm ($^1/_4$in) wide.

Cannelloni Pasta tubes 7–10cm (3–4in) long, generally filled, covered with sauce, and baked.

Spirali Also called rotelle, these are short, 5cm (2in) long, corkscrew-shaped pasta.

Macaroni Sometimes elbow-shaped, these are short, hollow tubes, baked with a cheese sauce.

Spaghetti Long, thin rod-like pasta made from white or wholewheat flour.

Thin spaghetti is called spaghettini.

Ravioli Usually fresh, square-shaped pasta stuffed with a meat, cheese or vegetable filling.

Tortellini Fresh white or spinach pasta filled with cheese, meat or other fillings, and formed into a ring-shaped dumpling.

Capelli d'Angelo Very fine, long strands of pasta, sometimes called "angel hair" pasta.

Penne rigate

Macaroni

Tagliatelle paglia e fieno

Spinach and ricotta tortellini (fresh)

Ravioli (fresh)

Angel hair spaghetti (fresh)

MAKING PASTA DOUGH: BASIC EGG PASTA

As with bread and pastry doughs, the amount of liquid the flour will hold depends on the type of flour.

INGREDIENTS

300g (10oz) plain or pasta flour
1 teaspoon salt
1 tablespoon oil (optional)
3 medium eggs, lightly beaten

1 Put flour and salt in a bowl or on a work surface. Stir to blend. Make a well in the centre and add the eggs, and, if using, oil.

2 With a fork or your fingertips, gradually incorporate the flour into the eggs until a soft dough forms. If the dough is very sticky, work in a little more flour.

3 Knead the dough on the work surface for about 8–10 minutes, until it is smooth and elastic. Add a little flour, if necessary.

4 Cover the dough with an upside down bowl. Allow to rest about 20 minutes. Alternatively, put the dough into a bowl, cover with cling film and refrigerate overnight or until ready to roll and shape.

COLOURED PASTA

Dried pastas are available in a variety of colours, but remember if colouring pasta at home, you may need to add a little more flour to the basic dough to compensate for the extra moisture.

Green pasta Add 350g (12oz) cooked fresh spinach or swiss chard, squeezed dry, and finely chopped with the eggs.

Red pasta Add 1–2 tablespoons tomato purée or finely chopped sun-dried tomatoes with the eggs; add 4 tablespoons carrot or red bell pepper purée with the eggs.

Beet pasta Add $1^1/_2$ tablespoons beetroot purée to the eggs.

Fresh herb pasta Add 2 tablespoons finely chopped parsley, basil, tarragon or cilantro with the eggs; if you like, add 1–2 cloves of finely chopped garlic with the eggs.

Lemon pasta Add $1^1/_2$ tablespoons grated rind and $^1/_2$ teaspoon lemon juice with the eggs.

Saffron or yellow pasta Add $^1/_2$ teaspoon ground saffron to the flour or steep a few saffron threads in 1 tablespoon hot water; add with the eggs.

Wholemeal pasta Replace 50–75g (2–3oz) white flour with the same quantity wholemeal flour.

ROLLING AND CUTTING PASTA DOUGH BY HAND

Cut the dough into thirds or quarters. Work with one piece at a time, keeping the remaining pieces covered to prevent drying out.

1 Using a long pasta rolling pin or extra-long rolling pin, begin from the centre, rolling out the dough on a lightly floured surface to a thickness of 0.3cm ($^1/_8$ in) – or thinner, if possible. If the dough becomes too elastic to handle, cover for a few minutes with a damp dish towel and let it rest.

2 If making pasta shapes, cut the shapes immediately while the dough is still soft and pliable. If hand-cutting noodles, dust lightly with flour and allow to dry slightly for about 10–20 minutes. (If machine cutting, allow to dry only about 5–10 minutes.)

TO CUT NOODLES BY HAND:

1 Loosely roll up dough and cut crosswise: 0.3cm ($^1/_8$in) for fettucine, 0.5cm ($^1/_4$in) for tagliatelle, 1cm ($^1/_2$in) for pappardelle or wide egg noodles.

2 Unroll the noodles and spread on a clean tea towel; sprinkle with a little flour or semolina and toss to prevent sticking. Alternatively, hang noodles on a special pasta drying rack, towel rack, or broom handle propped on two chair backs. Dry up to 2–3 hours before cooking. If not cooking immediately, refrigerate in layers, dusted with flour or semolina, in an airtight container.

ROLLING AND CUTTING PASTA DOUGH BY MACHINE

If you intend to make pasta regularly, it is worth investing in a pasta machine. In addition to rolling and cutting, it can knead the dough evenly beforehand.

1 To knead dough, set the machine rollers to the widest setting. Flour both rollers and the dough. Flatten the dough slightly before feeding it through the rollers, while turning the handle.

2 Fold the dough in thirds, folding the top third over, then the bottom third up over the top.

3 Feed it through again, open-side first through the rollers. Continue rolling and folding 6–8 times, flouring dough and rollers as necessary. This completes the kneading process.

ROLLING AND CUTTING PASTA DOUGH BY MACHINE CONTINUED

4 To roll and flatten the dough, narrow the rollers by one notch. Feed the dough strip through. Now do not fold the dough; narrow the rollers by one notch and feed the dough strip through again. Continue rolling and narrowing the gap between rollers until the dough is thin enough to be cut, about 0.3cm ($^1/_8$ in) or thinner. (The dough will be about 1 metre long.) Spread the dough on a surface, dust with flour, and allow to dry slightly, about 10–15 minutes. This will help prevent the dough from sticking to the rollers when cutting.

5 To cut the dough, lightly flour a baking sheet or tea cloth and set under the machine. Move the setting to the cutting roller or fit the cutting roller as directed. Feed the dough strip through, letting the cut noodles fall loosely onto the baking sheet or towel. Dust the noodles with a little more flour or semolina and store as for hand-cut noodles.

TO MAKE FILLED PASTA

Prepare the filling and roll the pasta extra thin, at least 0.2cm ($^1/_6$ in). Filled shapes will have a double thickness of pasta, so it must be rolled thin. About 450g (1lb) stuffing will fill about 25–30 shapes.

RAVIOLI:
1 Lay a dough strip on a lightly floured surface and cut crossways in half. Onto one half, drop $^1/_2$ teaspoon of the filling in vertical rows about 4cm ($1^1/_2$ in) apart.

2 Dip a pastry brush or your fingers sparingly in water and moisten the pasta dough around the filling.

3 Lay the other half of the dough strip on top. Press the dough sheets together between the mounds of filling.

4 Using a chef's knife or pasta or pizza wheel, first cut vertical, then horizontal lines between the filled squares. Using a fork, press to seal the edges of the filled pasta squares. Sprinkle with a little semolina to prevent sticking.

5 Alternatively, cut the ravioli with a round cutter or other shape and sprinkle as in step 4. Allow to dry slightly before cooking, or store up to 1 day as for fresh-cut noodles.

TORTELLINI:

1 Use a 7.5cm (3in) round cutter to make as many circles from the rolled-out pasta dough as possible. Put a teaspoon of filling in the centre of each and brush the dough edge with water.

2 Fold one side of the dough over to enclose the filling, making a half-moon shape. Press the edges together to seal well.

3 Moisten the ends on one side of the half moon. Curve the dough around your index finger, then pinch the moistened pointed ends together to seal them.

COOKING PASTA

Fresh pasta and dried pasta are cooked the same way, in plenty of boiling salted water. Allow about 4.2 litres (7 pints) of water for each 450g (1lb) of pasta. Use about 1 tablespoon salt for each 450 g 91lb) of pasta. If you like, add a tablespoon of oil to the water when it comes to the boil; some cooks say it helps to prevent the pasta from sticking to itself.

1 Bring a large pot of salted water to the rapid boil over high heat. Add the pasta and bring the water back to the boil as quickly as possible, stirring occasionally.

2 If cooking spaghetti, hold the spaghetti in one hand and push one end into the water slowly; it will begin to bend as it softens. Gradually push it completely into the water, stirring with a long-handled fork to separate.

3 When the water comes back to the boil, reduce the heat slightly and cook at a gentle boil. Follow the recommended cooking times on the package for dried pasta, but begin testing at the minimum end of the cooking time range. Thin pastas, like angel hair, can be cooked in 3 minutes, while rigatoni could take as long as 12 minutes. To test, use a slotted spoon to lift a piece of pasta out of the water. Run it under cold water and bite into it; it should be al dente or "firm to the tooth". Or, cut in half with a small sharp knife. It should look completely cooked with no opaque or uncooked dough in the centre.

4 To stop cooking, add a cup of cold water to the pasta pot. Then drain immediately in a colander.

5 Fresh pasta noodles cook in under a minute. Drop into the boiling water; they are cooked as soon as they float to the surface. Stuffed shapes take between 7–9 minutes, since there are two layers of pasta.

STORING PASTA

DRYING PASTA:
If fresh pasta is not used within an hour or two of making, it should be dried completely or it will become mouldy. Hang pasta for several hours on a special drying rack, towel rack, or a broom handle propped between 2 chairs.

NOODLES:
Curl cut noodles into nests while still soft. Lay on a floured baking sheet or tea towel to dry thoroughly. Arrange noodles in layers in a plastic box or container, sprinkled with semolina or cornmeal. Use greaseproof paper or baking parchment paper to separate layers and prevent sticking. Refrigerate up to 3 days.

FILLED PASTA:
Store filled pasta shapes on a baking sheet or in layers, sprinkled with semolina or cornmeal, for up to 1 day.

NOODLES AND DUMPLINGS

Asian and some other cultures use their pasta in the form of noodles. Noodles can be fresh or dried, with or without egg, made from wheat flour, soya bean flour or rice flour. Most are boiled like Mediterranean pasta, but some require soaking to soften for eating or frying.

Dumplings are small rounds of dough, sometimes leavened, poached in a simmering liquid such as water, stock or milk. Although generally easy to make, dumplings can be tricky to cook. If the recipe directs cooking covered, do not be tempted to uncover — re-covering causes the temperature to rise again, there is a risk they will overcook. Allow room for dumplings to expand and keep them at a simmer; boiling hard could cause them to break up.

NOODLE GLOSSARY

Cellophane noodles Made from mung-bean flour. Used in most oriental cuisines. Harusame, Japanese cellophane noodles, are made from rice flour. They need to be soaked before cooking.

Egg noodles Fresh egg noodles made from wheat flour and egg. They are the most commonly used noodles, from soups to stir-fries.

Rice noodles Thin white noodles, mostly sold dried in bundles. They need to be soaked for about 2 hours before boiling.

Rice papers Thin, dry, translucent circles used to make Thai- and Vietnamese-style spring rolls.

Rice sticks Ribbon-like rice noodles. Used in fried dishes.

Soba noodles Thin, flat, usually buckwheat noodles popular in Japanese "fast foods", like noodle soups. Can also be served cold with a dipping sauce.

Somen Fine, shiny, white Japanese wheat flour noodles which cook in 2–3 minutes. Served cold with a dipping sauce.

Udon Long, thin, ribbon-like Japanese wheat flour noodles.

Wheat noodles Chinese wheat flour noodles, made without eggs.

Wonton wrappers Wafer-thin wheat flour squares, about 7.5cm (3in) square, sold fresh or frozen.

Yifu noodles Round, yellow egg noodles, woven into a round cake. For use in soups and stir-fries.

Rice noodles

Rice paper

Soba noodles

Yifu noodles

Egg noodles

Wonton wrappers

MATZO BALLS (KNAIDLACH)

INGREDIENTS

4 eggs, lightly beaten
5 tablespoon margarine or vegetable fat, softened almost to melting
50ml (2 fl oz) chicken stock or water
1 teaspoon salt
$1/4$ teaspoon pepper
Pinch of cinnamon or nutmeg
115g (4oz) matzo meal

1 Beat eggs with the almost melted margarine or vegetable fat, the chicken stock or water, and the salt, pepper and cinnamon.

2 Stir in matzo meal until well blended. Cover and refrigerate about 1 hour. This allows the matzo meal to absorb the liquid and swell.

3 Using wet hands, shape the dough into 2cm ($3/4$ in) balls and drop into simmering soup or water. Cover and simmer about 20 minutes. Serve in soup.

PASTRY

Pastry is rich, unleavened dough made with flour, some kind of fat, and usually a liquid to bind the two together. All cooks aspire to making light, tender, flaky pastry. To achieve this goal, it is important to understand what each ingredient does and how it reacts, then to follow some basic rules in making and handling the dough.

MAKING PASTRY

There are three basic kinds of pastry – plain pastry, of which shortcrust or pie crust is the best known; puff pastry, the famous *pâte feuilletée* of *mille-feuille* (napoleons); and choux pastry, the basis for cream puffs and profiteroles.

Be careful not to overwork the dough or the pastry will be too tough. "Relaxing" the dough is essential for all pastries. Chilling the dough makes it easier to manage. Keep the ingredients and pastry chilled between each step of preparation for light, crispy pastry. With rich pastry, soften the dough at room temperature for 10–15 minutes, and lightly flour the rolling pin and work surface, for easier rolling.

PASTRY INGREDIENTS

Although there are limited ingredients in pastry, they can vary greatly, giving a variety of results. In pastry making, measuring accurately is paramount, and ingredients should be weighed rather than measured by volume, if possible.

Flour Flour is the most important ingredient. A soft wheat flour is best for pastry. Hard flours produce a firm, harder dough. Plain flour is used in most recipes. Wholemeal or rye flours produce a slightly heavier result. Use more white flour to wholemeal or other flours for easier handling.

Fat Fat provides the shortness in pastry, as well as its richness and flavour. The normal proportion is usually half fat to flour. The more fat the dough contains, the more difficult it will be to handle, so be sure to chill it after every stage.

Liquids Most pastry is bound with water, although milk or other liquids can be used. Use the minimum amount of liquid, as too much can make a sticky, hard-to-handle dough and a tough pastry. The water should be iced or very cold. The normal proportion is about 1 teaspoon water per 25g (1oz) of flour, but this will vary if whole eggs, yolks or other liquids are used.

Eggs Eggs or egg yolks are added to pastry for richness and flavour, and because they help bind the ingredients. Some rich doughs use only yolks with the fat and flour.

Salt and sugar Salt, as in many other preparations, helps to bring out the flavour of the other ingredients. Sugar sweetens pastry and gives it a crispier texture.

SHORTCRUST PASTRY (PÂTÉ BRISÉE)

Pâté Brisée, a basic pie crust, produces a firm, flaky crust which is supportive, yet tender. Brisée in French means broken; in this dough the flour and fats are "broken together" or rubbed in, as we say. Use half fat and half butter if you prefer, but remember the white fat will make the pastry shorter and more difficult to handle. If, after adding the liquid, the dough becomes sticky, refrigerate it. Sifting the flour is not necessary but can help lighten the pastry. The amount of pastry below is for a 22.5–25cm (9–10in) pie or tart tin.

INGREDIENTS

175g (6oz) plain flour
$^{1}/_{2}$ teaspoon salt
1 teaspoon sugar, optional
90g (3oz) cold unsalted butter or margarine, cut into small pieces
25g (1oz) cold margarine or shortening, cut into small pieces
2–4 tablespoons ice water

1 Sift the flour, salt and sugar, if using, into a large bowl. Sprinkle the pieces of fat over the flour mixture. Cut in the fat until the mixture forms coarse crumbs. Do not overwork or allow to become warm.

2 Sprinkle about 2 tablespoons water over the flour-crumb mixture and toss lightly with a fork. Gather together any pieces of dough which have "clumped" together. Add a little more water to the dry crumbs and toss again, continuing until the mixture is moist enough to stick together when pinched between your thumb and index finger.

3 Gather the dough into a rough ball and wrap with a sheet of cling film. Press the dough into a flat disk shape about 2.5cm (1in) thick. Wrap tightly and refrigerate at least 1 hour or overnight.

RICH SHORTCRUST PASTRY (PÂTÉ BRISÉE RICHE)

INGREDIENTS

175g (6oz) plain flour
$^{1}/_{2}$ teaspoon salt
1–2 teaspoons superfine sugar,
  optional
115g (4oz)) cold unsalted butter,
  cut into small pieces
1 egg yolk, beaten with 2
  tablespoons water

VARIATIONS

Light wholemeal crust Use 115g (4oz)
plain flour, 90g (3oz) wholemeal flour,
$^{1}/_{2}$ teaspoon salt, 40g (1$^{1}/_{2}$oz) cold
unsalted butter, cut up, 15g ($^{1}/_{2}$oz)
shortening or margarine, and egg yolk
beaten with 2 tablespoons ice water.

Light nut crust Add 2–3 tablespoons
finely chopped nuts to the flour.

Extra sweet crust This rich, melting
pastry can be tricky to handle; chill if it
becomes too sticky. If it is too difficult
to roll out, pat it into a pie plate or tart
pan using flour-dipped fingers. Use
140g (5oz) plain flour,
$^{1}/_{2}$ teaspoon salt, 4–5 tablespoons icing
sugar, 115g (4oz) cold unsalted butter,
cut into small pieces, 3 egg yolks
beaten with 1 tablespoon ice water, and
$^{1}/_{2}$ teaspoon vanilla essence.
Rich nut crust Ideal for custards and
cooked fillings, this dough can be

pressed straight into the pan without
rolling. Put 1 225g (8oz) room-
temperature unsalted butter, 1 lightly
beaten egg, 1 teaspoon vanilla or
almond essence (optional), 140g (5oz)
plain flour, $^{1}/_{2}$ teaspoon salt,
1–2 tablespoons sugar, and 115g (4oz)
finely chopped walnuts, pecans,
almonds, hazelnuts or macadamias into
the bowl of a food processor fitted with
the metal blade. Using the pulse button,
process until well-blended and smooth.
Alternatively beat in a large bowl with
an electric mixer until well-blended.

Crumb crust Popular for cheesecakes and
ice-cream pies, this is easy to make. Put
115g (4oz) crumbled digestive biscuits or
other biscuits in the bowl of a food
processor and process until fine crumbs
form. Add 90g (3oz) melted butter and 1–2
tablespoons sugar (optional) and process
to blend. Press onto a springform pan or
pie plate and chill.

ROLLING PIE CRUST PASTRY: TO FORM A DOUGH CIRCLE

For rich pastry soften the dough at room temperature for 10–15 minutes. Lightly flour the work surface and the rolling pin.

1 Use a lightly floured rolling pin to press a row of parallel grooves into the dough circle. Turn the dough 45°, lightly flouring the surface underneath. Press another row of parallel grooves. Continue rotating and pressing the dough until it is about 1cm (½ in) thick.

2 Beginning from the centre, lightly roll out the dough to the far edge, but do not actually roll over the edge. Return to the centre and roll to the nearest edge, but do not roll over the edge. Rotate the dough 45° and continue rolling until the dough is about 0.3-cm (⅛-in) thick and forms a circle about 30cm (12in). Lightly flour the surface and the rolling pin as needed.

3 Use a small pastry brush to remove excess flour from the dough. Patch any tears with a small piece of moistened dough.

4 As the dough gets bigger, fold it in half or quarters to rotate, or roll it over the rolling pin to dust the surface with flour; this avoids stretching or tearing very fragile doughs.

5 Use a tart tin or inverted pie plate as a guide to trim the dough 5cm (2in) larger all around than the tin or plate.

TO FORM A SQUARE:
Proceed as for a dough circle, but rotate the dough 90° instead of 45° when pressing in the grooves. This will cause the dough to elongate to fill a square pan.

TO FREEZE ROLLED-OUT PASTRY

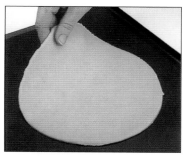

1 Carefully slide onto a flat baking sheet and open-freeze until very firm. Slide the frozen dough shape onto freezer paper, wrap tightly, and freeze.

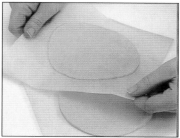

2 Or, freeze several with layers of freezer paper between each. Defrost in the refrigerator overnight or for several hours at room temperature before using.

BUSY COOKS

The food processor is the answer to your prayers if you have warm hands, a heavy touch, or just don't have the knack – just be careful not to overprocess.

1 Put the flour, salt and sugar into the bowl of a food processor fitted with the metal blade. Process 5 seconds to blend. Sprinkle the fat over the flour mixture and, using the pulse button, process until the mixture resembles coarse crumbs.

2 Remove the cover and sprinkle 2 tablespoons of the water over the flour mixture. Using the pulse button, process 10–15 seconds until the mixture just begins to hold together – *do not overprocess*. Test the dough by pinching between your fingers. If the dough is too crumbly, add a little more water, little by little, and pulse again. Do not allow dough to form into a ball or add too much water, or the pastry will be tough.

PUFF PASTRY

1 Cut the butter into tiny pieces. Set on a plate, spread evenly, and freeze for 30 minutes. While the butter freezes, chill your work surface with a roasting pan or baking tray filled with ice cubes.

INGREDIENTS

200g (7oz) unsalted butter
275g (9³/₄oz) plain flour
1 tablespoon cornflour
1 teaspoon salt
125–175ml (4–6 fl oz) very cold
    whipping cream or half cream
    and half ice water

2 Put the flour, cornflour and salt in the bowl of a food processor fitted with the metal blade. Using the pulse button, process 5–7 seconds to blend. Sprinkle over the frozen butter and process 3–4 times; the butter will still be in lumps.

4 Turn onto a piece of plastic wrap and form into a ball. Flatten to a disk shape and wrap. Chill 20 minutes.

5 Lightly flour a work surface and roll out the dough to a long rectangle at least 3 times longer than it is wide (about 15 x 45cm/6 x 18in). Brush off any excess flour.

3 Remove the cover and evenly pour in 125ml (4 fl oz) of the cream, water, or a mixture of the two. Process 5 seconds; the mixture should look lumpy, and stick together when pinched between your thumb and index finger. If the dough is dry or crumbly, add a little more liquid, and pulse just enough to blend.

6 Fold the bottom third of the rectangle up and the top third down over the bottom third, as if folding a letter. Brush off any excess flour.

7 Press edge down with the rolling pin to seal. Rotate the dough a quarter turn with one open seam facing toward you and the other away from you. Roll out to the same long rectangle and fold into thirds again.

8 Press the edges together with the rolling pin. Press your 1st and 2nd fingers into the top to make two indentations to indicate 2 "turns". Wrap dough tightly and refrigerate 30 minutes.

9 Remove from the refrigerator; roll and fold the dough two more times, making four indentations to indicate four turns. Wrap tightly for another $1/2$ hour before using, or chill up to 3 days.

CREAM PUFF PASTRY

INGREDIENTS

140g (5oz) plain flour, sifted
225ml (8 fl oz) water
1 teaspoon sugar
$^1/_2$ teaspoon salt
125g (4oz) unsalted butter, cut into
   small pieces
3–4 eggs

1 Preheat the oven to 220°C (425°F/Gas 7). Lightly grease a large baking sheet. Put the water, sugar, salt and butter into a medium saucepan and bring to the boil over medium heat; the butter should be completely melted just as the water comes to a boil. (This is very important; the water should not continue boiling to melt the butter, or the proportions of the ingredients could alter.)

2 As soon as the water boils and the butter is melted, remove the pan from heat. Add the flour mixture all at once and beat vigorously with a wooden spoon; the dough will form into a ball and pull away from the sides of the pan.

3 Return pan to the heat and continue to beat for about 1 minute to dry out dough as much as possible without scorching it. Remove from the heat and cool slightly.

4 Beat in three eggs, one at a time, beating well. At first the mixture seems to repel the egg, then it is slowly absorbed. Beat the fourth egg lightly with a fork and add it, little by little, just until the dough is smooth, shiny and soft enough to fall from the spoon.

5 To form into cream puffs, use 2 spoons to shape rounds. Drop onto the prepared baking sheet at least 5cm (2in) apart.

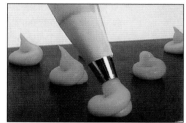

6 Alternatively, spoon the pastry dough into a large pastry bag fitted with a 2-cm ($^3/_4$-in) plain tip. Pressing evenly, pipe into mounds or eclair shapes, or as recipe directs.

7 Brush with a little egg wash and use a dampened fork to smooth the tops. Bake 15 minutes, then reduce the temperature to 202°C (400°F). Continue to bake 15–20 minutes longer, with the door slightly open. Bake until well puffed and golden brown.

8 Remove the baking sheet to a wire rack. Carefully pierce a hole to make a slit in the sides of the puffs or eclairs to allow the steam to escape. Return to the oven for 5–10 minutes to dry out. Remove to a wire rack to cool completely.

9 To fill the cream puffs, slice each one horizontally. Remove any uncooked or soggy dough. Spoon whipped cream or pastry cream into the bottom half of each puff and cover with the top half. Dust with icing sugar or top with chocolate sauce.

BREAD AND CAKES

Making bread is a comforting and rewarding experience. Once you understand how to capitalize on the characteristics of flour and yeast, a beautiful, well-textured loaf of bread will be part of your standard baking repertoire. Throughout the world cakes have a long-standing tradition and are often the centrepiece of many special occasions, from birthdays to weddings to christenings, as well as of many holidays.

MAKING BREAD

The simplest breads are made of flour, water, yeast and salt. Adding egg, sugar, milk, butter, nuts, raisins or other ingredients will produce richer, sweeter, more cake-like breads. Using other flours, such as wholemeal or rye, cornmeal or oats, adds texture to the dough.

The gluten content and the consistency of flour varies from region to region, season to season, and even batch to batch. Therefore, the amount of liquid any flour absorbs will vary. Gluten, a form of protein, absorbs liquid and produces elastic strands in the dough.

Yeast is the rising agent used in most breadmaking. Proofing the yeast – the first step in breadmaking – ensures that the yeast is active and begins the initial fermentation. Kneading, the most important step, distributes the yeast evenly throughout the dough. Kneaded dough needs to rise at least once, sometimes twice, depending on the dough and the type of yeast.

Salt slows down the yeast's fermentation. It helps to control the rising of the dough, as well as accenting flavor. Generally, a scant tablespoon for each 450g (1lb) flour is about right.

Liquid binds the dough and begins the fermentation of the yeast. Water is most commonly used, but milk gives a softer texture.

USING YEAST

Yeast is very sensitive to temperature, thriving at about 80°F (27.5°C). At lower temperatures, it works more slowly or becomes dormant; at temperatures above 59°F (138°C) it dies. It is available in two forms: compressed – also called fresh or cake yeast – and active dry yeast. Compressed yeast is more perishable and can be difficult to find. It should be a creamy beige colour and have a sweet, fresh, yeasty smell. If it has a dark appearance or spots or a sour smell, discard it. Compressed yeast can be refrigerated, well-wrapped, up to 2 weeks. It is available in 15g (1oz) cubes and 450-g (1-lb) blocks, and can be frozen up to a month. Active dry yeast is easily available and can be stored for months in a cool, dry place, although it is best stored in the refrigerator.

EASY WHITE BREAD

1 Put yeast in a small bowl, stir in the warm water, add a little of the sugar, and stir to dissolve.

2 Set aside until yeast is "proofed", when fermentation causes puffing and frothing around the edge of the liquid. If it does not proof at all, discard it and start again.

3 Meanwhile, heat milk to about 42°C (110°F) and stir in butter until it is completely melted. Set aside until it is the same temperature as the yeast mixture.

INGREDIENTS

1 scant tablespoon) active dry yeast
4 tablespoons warm water (42°–44.5°C/110°–115°F)
1–2 tablespoons sugar
225ml (8 fl oz) warm milk (42°–44.5°C/110°–115°F)
40g (1$^{1}/_{2}$oz) butter, diced
450g (1lb) all-purpose flour, plus extra
1 tablespoon salt
1 egg, beaten with 1 tablespoon water for glaze

4 Sift flour, salt, and remaining sugar into a large bowl, stirring to combine. Using a large spoon, make a well in the centre. Add "proofed" yeast mixture.

5 Pour the milk and butter mixture into the bowl.

6 Using a wooden spoon, gradually draw flour from the edge of the well into the liquid.

7 Continue until a soft dough forms and pulls away from the side of the bowl. If dough is too wet and sticky, sprinkle over a little more flour, a tablespoon at a time. If it is too dry, add a little more warm water.

8 Turn dough onto a lightly floured work surface. Begin to knead it. Fold dough onto itself, pulling towards you, then push it away from you with the heel of your hand.

9 Rotate dough a quarter turn, repeating the action. Continue for about 10 minutes, adding a little flour from time to time, if necessary, until dough is smooth and elastic, and air bubbles form on the surface.

10 Shape dough into a ball, transfer to a large oiled bowl, and cover. Or slide it into a large plastic freezer bag, oiled inside, and seal. Set bowl in a warm draft-free place, about 24°–27°C (75°–80°F), for 1 to 1¹/₂ hours, until double in bulk.

11 To test if dough has risen sufficiently, push 2 fingers about 2.5cm (1in) into it. If dough does not spring back, it is ready.

12 Punch or knock back dough by pushing a fist into the center to deflate it. Turn onto a lightly floured surface, knead lightly 1–2 minutes, and shape into a ball. Let it rest about 5 minutes. Meanwhile, lightly butter or oil two 20 x 10 x 5-cm (8 x 4 x 2-in) loaf pans.

13 Using a sharp knife, cut dough in half. Form into two 20-cm (8-in) rectangles, gently stretching and rounding the edges. Tuck long ends under and drop each loaf into a pan. Cover pans with a clean, dry tea towel or slide into a large plastic bag and seal.

14 Set in a warm place to rise again, 45 minutes to 1 hour, or until double in bulk. Preheat the oven to 230°C (450°F/Gas 8).

15 Brush tops with egg glaze and bake in the center of the oven 15 minutes. Reduce to 190°C (375°F/Gas 5) and bake 20 to 25 minutes longer, until tops are well browned.

16 To test to see if it is done, turn a loaf out and tap the bottom with your knuckles: it should sound hollow. For a crisper loaf, remove loaves from their pans and bake on the rack 5 to 10 minutes longer.

SHAPING OTHER LOAVES

Other free-form shapes are easy to create with most classic bread doughs. Be sure to grease baking sheets or other pans.

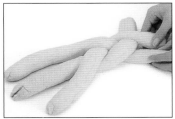

FREE-FORM ROUND:
1 For one large loaf: shape kneaded dough into a ball, gently pulling side under centre to form a tighter ball.

2 Place the ball on a prepared baking sheet seam side down. Using a sharp knife, slash top with an "X".

PLAITED LOAF:
1 Cut dough into three equal pieces. Roll each piece to a long rope shape, tapering the ends. Lie rope shapes next to each other. Beginning in the centre and working towards one end, plait ropes together.

2 Pinch ends together and tuck them under the plait. Turn dough and continue plaiting the other end, pinching ends and tucking under. Transfer to a baking sheet, keeping ends tucked under.

MAKING PIZZA DOUGH

Pizza dough generally has a higher proportion of yeast to flour and so rises more quickly. This dough makes a large round pizza or can be baked in a 38.25 x 26cm (15^1/$_2$ x 10^1/$_2$-in) Swiss roll tin.

1 Pour about 4 tablespoons warm water into a small bowl, sprinkle with yeast, and stir with a fork to dissolve. Allow to stand 10–15 minutes to "proof", stirring occasionally.

2 Sift flour and salt together into a large bowl. Make a well in the centre. Pour in the "proofed" yeast, olive oil and remaining water.

INGREDIENTS

1 scant tablespoon) active dry yeast
225ml (8 fl oz) warm water (43°C/110°F)
2^1/$_2$ cups (556 g) bread or plain flour
1^1/$_2$ teaspoons salt
3 tablespoons olive oil

3 Using a wooden spoon or your fingers, gradually draw in flour from the edge of the well, stirring until a soft dough forms and all the flour is incorporated. Allow the dough to rest about 2 minutes.

4 Turn the dough onto a lightly floured surface. Knead about 5 minutes, until dough is smooth and elastic. Shape into a ball and put into a large oiled bowl. Cover tightly and put in a warm (27°C/80°F) place to rise for about 1 hour.

5 Gently punch down dough and turn onto a lightly floured surface. Knead lightly for about 1 minute.

6 Roll out dough to a large circle about 0.5cm (^{1}/$_4$in) thick or a rectangular shape to fit the pan. Transfer to an oiled baking sheet or the oiled Swiss roll tin. Cover with desired topping to within 2cm (^{3}/$_4$in) of the edge. Allow to rise about 10 minutes, then bake as directed. The edge of the pizza crust should be puffed and browned.

TEA BREADS AND MUFFINS

Quick to make and bake, tea breads are raised without yeast, using baking powder, bicarbonate of soda or sometimes a combination of the two. They have a soft, crumbly, cake-like texture. The chemical raising agents used react quickly with moisture and heat, causing the doughs to rise. The most popular tea breads are loaf-style versions such as banana bread and nut breads. Bran and blueberry muffins are also favourites. Other types of tea breads include biscuits, scones, coffeecakes, cornbreads and batters used to produce pancakes, waffles and popovers.

BICARBONATE OF SODA, BAKING POWDER AND CREAM OF TARTARE

Mixing an acid and alkali to raise dough began during the Industrial Revolution. Commercial leaveners were first marketed in the 1850s.

Bicarbonate of soda combines with other acid ingredients such as buttermilk, sour cream, lemon juice, honey or molasses to create carbon dioxide bubbles which raise the dough. This action begins almost immediately. Once in the oven, the gas is released, and the dough doubles in volume before it cooks and sets. Bicarbonate of soda can also be activated by combining it with cream of tartare (an acid in powder form), then adding a liquid.

Baking powder is a combination of bicarbonate of soda and an acid salt, usually cream of tartare. (Cream of tartaer, an acid salt of tartaric acid, is a byproduct of wine-making.) Most baking powder is double-acting; this powder begins to react as soon as liquid is added, then again when heated. For this reason, doughs must be mixed and placed in the oven immediately.

Chemical raising agents should be stored in a cool, dark, dry place. Baking powder should be replaced every three to four months.

TEA BREADS: BANANA BREAD

1 Preheat oven to 160°C (325°FGas 3). Grease and flour an 22 x 11-cm (8^1/$_2$ x 4^1/$_2$-in) loaf tin. Sift together the flours, bicarbonate of soda, cinnamon, ginger and salt. Set aside.

INGREDIENTS

115g (4oz) plain flour
115g (4oz) wholemeal flour
1 teaspoon bicarbonate of soda
^{1}/$_2$ teaspoon ground cinnamon
^{1}/$_2$ teaspoon ground ginger
^{1}/$_2$ teaspoon salt
115g (4oz) butter, at room temperature
175g (6oz) superfine sugar
3 ripe bananas, mashed
2 eggs, lightly beaten
5 tablespoons hot water
90g (3oz) pecans, chopped

2 Using an electric mixer, beat butter until softened. Gradually beat in sugar until mixture is light and fluffy. Slowly beat in bananas and then the eggs. If the mixture looks curdled, add a little flour mixture.

3 Add flour mixture alternately with the hot water in 4–5 batches. Beat until smooth. Stir in the nuts.

4 Pour the mixture into prepared tin, smoothing the top.

5 Bake about 1 hour, until a cake tester inserted in the centre comes out clean. Cool in the tin 10 minutes, then turn on to a wire rack to cool.

CAKE-MAKING

Perfect cake-making depends on good ingredients, the correct utensils, careful measuring, accurate temperatures and exact timing.

Most cakes are batter mixtures of flour, fat, sugar, eggs, liquid and flavourings. Air or gas, introduced in the form of a leavening agent, makes the mixture rise while baking. Heating the gas makes the strands of gluten in the flour stretch until the cake sets. Even rising produces the characteristic spongy texture we prize so much.

There are five basic methods of cake-making. Sometimes a combination of two is used in preparing one cake. Whatever your choice of preparation, selecting and preparing the cake tin is very important. The type of tin will affect the baking time as well as the finish of the cake. A dark metal tin will reduce the cooking time slightly and encourage a darker crust; a tin with a drop-out base will help unmold fragile or delicate cakes; a spring-release tin is a necessity for cheesecakes, tortes (nut-based cakes) and cakes which, for any other reason, cannot be unmoulded. A heavy-based cake tin prevents long-cooking fruitcakes from scorching on the bottom. Use the size and shape of pan directed in the recipe.

GRANULATED VERSUS CASTER SUGAR

Many cakes and fine baked goods call for granulated sugar. Caster sugar can be more expensive, but dissolves more quickly and easily in fragile mixtures and in batters such as a whisked layer cake or in buttercream. To make caster sugar from granulated sugar, put the granulated sugar in the bowl of a food processor fitted with the metal blade and process for 20 seconds.

EGGS FOR CAKES

Eggs for cakes, as well as other baked goods, should always be at room temperature. Cold eggs may cause the butter and sugar mixture to curdle. The batter can be used, but the texture of the cake will not be as good. If the egg-sugar mixture appears curdled when beaten, sprinkle in about a tablespoon of the measured flour; it will help to bind it.

LEMON POUND CAKE

In this method the butter – or margarine – and sugar are creamed or beaten together to form a light, almost mousse-like consistency. Be sure to soften the butter to room temperature and use eggs and liquid at room temperature. Although a raising agent is usually added to ensure rising, it is the beating of the eggs which incorporates air and makes a light yet rich, moist cake.

1 Prepare an 20 x 10 x 5cm (8 x 4 x 2in) loaf pan as directed. Preheat oven to 170°C (325°F). Sift together flour, baking powder, and salt; set aside.

INGREDIENTS

225g (8oz) plain flour
2 teaspoons baking powder
$1/_4$ teaspoon salt
225g (8oz) unsalted butter, softened
175g (6oz) caster sugar
1 teaspoon grated lemon zest (optional)
4 eggs, lightly beaten
$1/_2$ teaspoon vanilla essence
1 teaspoon lemon essence

2 Beat butter until soft in a large bowl with a wooden spoon, or an electric mixer at medium speed. Gradually add sugar and continue beating at high speed until mixture is very light, moussy and pale in colour. Scrape down the side of the bowl occasionally.

3 Add the beaten eggs, a little at a time, beating well after each addition and scraping down the side of the bowl occasionally. If mixture begins to curdle, sprinkle over a little of the measured flour to help bind the mixture.

4 Add the dry ingredients in three batches, folding in lightly by hand until just blended. (The mixer can be used, but be careful not to overbeat). Any liquid required can be added at this point. Stir in gently, alternating with dry ingredients.

5 Spoon or lightly scrape the mixture into the prepared pan. Smooth the top and make a slight indentation in the centre. (This helps the cake to rise more evenly, as the centre usually puffs up more than the edges.)

6 Bake for 50–60 minutes, until the centre springs back when touched. Cool 10 minutes before unmoulding.

7 Dust with icing sugar before serving.

ALL-IN-ONE METHOD: SIMPLE SPONGE

This method is a variation of the creamed method, but all the ingredients are mixed and beaten in one step. The classic Victoria layer cake can be made by this method.

INGREDIENTS

175g (6oz) self-raising flour
1 teaspoon baking powder
$^1/_4$ teaspoon salt
175g (6oz) caster sugar
175g (6oz) unsalted butter, softened
3 eggs
1 teaspoon vanilla essence

1   Prepare two 17.5-cm (7-in) cake tins. Preheat oven to 180°C (350°F/Gas 4). Sift flour, baking powder and salt into a large bowl.

2   Add sugar, butter, eggs and vanilla essence. Beat with an electric mixer until smooth and well blended.

3   Pour into prepared tins and bake about 20 minutes. Cool and unmould as directed. Sandwich with freshly whipped cream and strawberry jam. Dust the top with icing sugar before serving.

MELTING METHOD: DARK GINGERBREAD

Cakes made by this method are usually rich in sugar or syrups and have a dense, moist texture. The fat is melted with the sugar, syrup and any other liquids, and cooled before the dry ingredients and eggs are stirred in. Bicarbonate of soda is usually the raising agent. Fruitcakes, gingerbreads and some chiffon cakes are made by this method.

1 Line an 20-cm (8-in) cake tin. Pre-heat oven to 160°C (325°F/Gas 3). Sift flour, salt, soda and ginger into a bowl.

2 Assemble the butter, corn syrup, molasses, brown sugar and preserved ginger.

INGREDIENTS

225g (8oz) plain flour
$^1/_4$ teaspoon salt
1 teaspoon bicarbonate of soda
1 tablespoon ground ginger
115g (4oz) butter
125ml (4 fl oz) corn syrup
125 ml (4 fl oz) molasses
115g (4oz) preserved ginger, finely chopped, or 1 teaspoon ground ginger
60g (2oz) dark brown sugar
2 eggs, lightly beaten
175ml (6 fl oz) milk

3 Combine them over medium-low heat until melted, stirring occasionally. Remove from heat and cool. Beat eggs and milk into the cooled mixture.

4 Make a well in the centre of the flour mixture and pour in the liquid mixture, stirring until smooth and well blended.

5 Bake about 1 hour, until a cake tester or skewer inserted in the centre comes out clean. Cool 10 minutes in the tin before unmoulding.

RUBBED-IN METHOD: MARMALADE LOAF

This is an old-fashioned method which produces a substantial cake with a moist texture, similar to a tea bread. The butter is rubbed into the flour as in pastry making, and the raising agent is bicarbonate of soda.

INGREDIENTS

225g (8oz) self-raising flour
$^1/_2$ teaspoon salt
115g (4oz) cold butter, diced
50g (2oz) caster sugar
2 eggs, lightly beaten
3 tablespoons orange marmalade
3 tablespoons milk

1 Prepare and line the bottom of an 20 x 10 x 5cm (8 x 4 x 2-in) loaf tin. Preheat oven to 180°C (350°F/Gas 4). Sift flour and salt into a large bowl.

2 Add diced butter to flour and toss to coat with flour. Using a pastry blender or your fingertips, rub in butter until the mixture resembles medium-fine breadcrumbs.

3 Stir in sugar, eggs, marmalade and milk until the mixture is well blended. Turn into the tin and bake about 50 minutes until a skewer comes out clean. Cool 10 minutes before unmoulding.

WHISKED METHOD

This method of cake-making contains no rising agents; the light, airy texture relies on the air beaten into the eggs. As the air expands in the heated oven, the cake rises. The most famous example of this cake is the French Genoise. Originally made with no fat at all, this whisked layer cake generally has a little melted butter folded into the batter at the end to enrich the cake and provide extra moisture. It is the basis for many famous cakes, Swiss rolls and desserts, but because it tends to be slightly dry, it is usually brushed with a flavoured sugar syrup or liqueur and is best eaten on the day made. It also makes the perfect vehicle for a rich buttercream icing.

This cake can be made by whisking whole eggs or by separating the eggs and whisking the yolks with the sugar as a base, then folding in the separately beaten whites with the flour at the end. This is called a "biscuit" mixture and has a slightly drier and firmer texture.

TO THE "RIBBON" STAGE
Whichever of the methods is used, the whole eggs or yolks and sugar are whisked, sometimes over heat to increase volume. When the whisk is lifted out of the bowl, the mixture should fall, leaving a "ribbon-like" trail on the surface of the mixture. If made with yolks only, the egg mixture will be thicker and more dense.

Beat eggs or yolks by hand with sugar in a stainless steel or other heatproof bowl, using a large balloon whisk. Set the bowl over, but not touching, a saucepan of just simmering (*not* boiling) water. Beat with an electric whisk at medium speed until the mixture is very pale and thick, forming a ribbon-trail when held over the bowl. This will take about 10 minutes. Remove from the heat and continue beating until cool.

ADDING THE BUTTER
Some recipes for whisked cakes do contain butter. If not added carefully, it can deflate the mixture, resulting in a heavy cake. Some cooks prefer the batter to be pourable, but still creamy, in which case the butter is melted. In that case, it should be completely cooled before being folded into the batter with the last portion of flour.

1 Before the last portion of flour is added, stir some batter into the melted butter to lighten it. Carefully fold the butter mixture into the batter.

2 Alternatively, cream butter until it is almost liquid, about the consistency of cream, but not clear or melted. Dribble it around the edge of the bowl and gently fold into batter. (Dumping it on to the surface will result in deflated batter.)

CLASSIC SPONGE CAKE

INGREDIENTS

115g (4oz) plain flour
$^1/_4$ teaspoon salt
4 eggs
115g (4oz) caster sugar
$^1/_2$ teaspoon vanilla or lemon essence
50g (2oz) butter, melted (optional)

1 Prepare and line the bottom of a 23-cm (9-in) cake tin. Sift flour with salt, then sift again. (This is best done over a large sheet of paper or a large bowl.)

2 Whisk eggs and sugar to the ribbon stage (see page 213). Add vanilla essence; beat until cool. Sift flour over the mixture in 2 or 3 batches and fold in as gently as possible.

3 If using melted butter, drizzle around the edge of the bowl and fold in with the last batch of flour. Pour into pan and bake about 25 minutes, until centre springs back when touched lightly with a fingertip. Cool for 10 minutes before unmoulding.

CHEESECAKE: CLASSIC NEW YORK STYLE

Not technically a cake, this is a popular confection made with curd, cream cheese or ricotta cheese. Usually baked in a spring-release tin lined with a crumb crust, or sometimes a pastry case, it does not have the texture of a cake, but is soft and moist. Eggs added to a creamed batter of cheese, sugar and flavourings set the mixture, rather than making it rise. Some cheesecakes are set with gelatine and chilled unbaked.

INGREDIENTS

23-cm (9-in) spring-release tin, lined with a
   baked crust
450g (1lb) full-fat soft cheese
300g (10oz) sugar
450ml (16 fl oz) soured cream
3 eggs
1 tablespoon vanilla essence

1 Beat cream cheese with an electric mixer, on low speed, until soft and creamy. Gradually beat in half the sugar until smooth and well blended. Beat in 125ml (4 fl oz) of the soured cream, and the eggs one at a time. Scrape down the side of the bowl occasionally. Beat in 2 teaspoons of the vanilla essence.

2 Bake in a preheated oven 160°C (325°F/Gas 4) for about 45 minutes. Reduce heat if the cake browns too quickly. Cool 5 minutes. Beat remaining soured cream with remaining sugar and vanilla. Pour over cheesecake and bake 5–7 minutes longer. Cool on a wire rack. Refrigerate overnight.

PERFECT CHEESECAKE
The most common cause of cracks is baking at too high a temperature; in this case the outside edge sets before the centre expands and settles. Baking in a water bath (wrap the tin in foil to prevent leaking) or setting a pan of water on the floor of the oven should help.

Overbeating can be another cause, or removing the cake from a hot oven to a cold surface. To combat this, underbake by 5 minutes, turn the oven off, open the door a crack, and let the cheesecake cool for an hour before removing from the oven.

CHOCOLATE

Chocolate is probably the world's favourite sweet flavouring, used as a filling as well as in truffles, fudge and sauces. Decorations, curls, leaves and ribbons also make the most of chocolate's universal appeal.

TYPES OF CHOCOLATE

Chocolate is found in many popular guises; from solid to pre-melted, dark through white, deeply brown and bitter to milky and sweet; even powdered, as cocoa. Chocolates owe their different tastes to the quality and roasting of the beans, the style of production, and the national preferences of the country in which the chocolate was manufactured.

Brand name chocolate is made from chocolate liquor blended with additional cocoa butter, sugar, and flavourings. The more chocolate liquor and cocoa butter the chocolate contains, the better the quality. Every country of production sets minimum standards. Although certain types of chocolate lend themselves to particular preparations, even that can be very much a personal preference.

Plain, bittersweet, and semisweet chocolate This dark chocolate varies from bittersweet to the slightly sweet plain and semisweet chocolate. It contains only chocolate liquor, cocoa butter and sometimes lecithin (an emulsifier) and sugar in varying quantities.

White chocolate Technically, white chocolate is not chocolate at all because it does not contain any chocolate liquor. It is becoming more popular and is used in cakes, mousses, sauces and desserts, and as a contrast with other chocolates.

Milk chocolate Milk chocolate has a lower cocoa solid content, about 15 per cent, and has dried milk powder added. This, and its much milder flavour, means that it cannot be substituted for bittersweet, dark or semisweet chocolate in baking and dessert recipes.

MELTING CHOCOLATE

There are several ways of melting chocolate, but no matter what method is used, it should be melted slowly. Chocolate can be melted on its own in a double saucepan, in the microwave, or in a very low oven. Remember, melted chocolate should feel *warm*, not hot.

Adding a liquid helps prevent chocolate from burning, but you must add enough to avoid seizing. Seizing is when the chocolate becomes grainy and firms up, looking like a dull, thick paste. Chocolate marries well with butter, cream, milk, water, coffee or a liqueur, and generally 1 tablespoon of liquid for every 50g (2oz) of chocolate is sufficient.

ON A STOVE:
To melt chocolate on its own on top of the stove, put the chocolate in the top of a double boiler or in a bowl set over very hot, simmering water. The base of the pan or bowl should not touch the water. Allow the chocolate to stand several minutes to soften, then begin to stir occasionally until it begins to melt. Stir until completely melted and smooth.

WITH A LIQUID OVER DIRECT HEAT:
Put the chopped or broken pieces of chocolate in a heavy-based saucepan. Add the measured amount of liquid or butter. Set over low heat and stir frequently, until melted and smooth. Remove from the heat.

TO "LOOSEN" SEIZED CHOCOLATE:
Stir in about 1 teaspoon white vegetable fat or oil for each 25 g (1oz) of chocolate. Do not use butter or margarine because they contain water. If it does not work, start again with new chocolate. Do not discard the seized chocolate, however; it can be used in a recipe which melts chocolate in another liquid.

TEMPERING CHOCOLATE

"Tempering" is a process of slowly heating and cooking chocolate to stabilize the emulsified cocoa solids and cocoa fat. It is generally used by professionals in recipes that require *couverture* chocolate, which shrinks quickly for easy release from moulds, and can be kept at room temperature for weeks without losing its crispness and shiny surface. Untempered chocolate should be refrigerated immediately to solidify the cocoa butter and prevent it from rising to the surface causing fat bloom.

All solid chocolate is tempered in production, but once melted it loses its "temper" and must be retempered.

1 Melt the couverture chocolate by one of the methods on the left. The temperature should be about 42°C (110°F); check with an instant-read or sugar thermometer. Stir to be sure the chocolate is completely melted and smooth.

2 Pour about three-quarters of the chocolate onto a marble slab or work surface. Using a metal palette knife or rubber scraper, scrape into a pool in the centre, then spread out again. Work the chocolate in this way for 3–5 minutes until no streaks remain.

3 Scrape the chocolate back into the bowl and stir into the remaining chocolate until well blended. The temperature should now be 32°C (90°F). The chocolate is tempered and ready for use.

COATING WITH CHOCOLATE

Candy and small pieces of fruit can be coated in chocolate. Using tempered chocolate is ideal, but melted plain chocolate also can be used if it is refrigerated after cooking until needed.

1 Melt (or remelt) the chocolate and pour into a deep bowl. The temperature should be between 44.5–47°C (115–120°F). Use a special chocolate dipping fork, skewer or fondue fork to lower the candy or fruit into the chocolate.

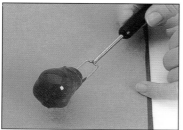

2 Turn to coat completely, then lift out of the melted chocolate. Tap gently and scrape on the edge of the bowl to remove the excess chocolate.

3 Set on a baking sheet lined with baking parchment. Draw the tines of the dipping fork across the top, lifting lightly, to leave two raised edges.

CHOCOLATE LEAVES

Use any fresh, non-toxic leaves with prominent veins, such as rose or lemon. Using a pastry brush, brush melted chocolate over the veined side of a leaf, coating evenly and completely. Set on a paper-lined baking sheet and refrigerate to set. Starting at the stem end, gently peel away the leaf.

EASY CHOCOLATE TRUFFLES

Simple chocolate truffles are surprisingly easy to make. Roll in cocoa or chopped nuts, or coat with tempered chocolate and decorate more elaborately.

INGREDIENTS

225g (8oz) fine-quality plain chocolate, chopped
90ml (3 fl oz) double cream
1–2 tablespoons brandy or rum
cocoa powder for rolling

1 Melt the chocolate in a double boiler or in a bowl set over hot water. Alternatively, use a microwave.
2 Remove the melted chocolate from the heat and stir in the cream until well blended. Cool to room temperature and stir in the brandy and rum. Refrigerate until the mixture is firm enough to shape – about 30 minutes.

3 Stir a little cocoa into a small bowl or shallow plate. Shape teaspoonfuls of the truffle mixture into balls, rolling gently between your fingers or palms.

4 Roll the balls in the cocoa to coat completely. Use a fork or slotted spoon to remove from the coating, tapping off any excess. Set on a baking sheet and repeat with remaining mixture. Refrigerate until ready to eat.

INDEX